HELP FROM HEAVEN

To Maria.
El amor de Dios
esta dentro de ti.
tu brillas con luz
propia.
Recuerda no estas
sola, tus angeles
Guardianes estan
contigo, pide
ayuda cuando
la necesites
estaremos alli
Paz y amor
Clamos
Vivas

HELP FROM HEAVEN

MIRACLES HAPPEN WHEN YOU BELIEVE

CARLOS VIVAS

NEW DEGREE PRESS

COPYRIGHT © 2021 CARLOS VIVAS

Unless otherwise indicated, Bible verses are taken from the King James Version (KJV), Public Domain.

HELP FROM HEAVEN
Miracles Happen When You Believe

ISBN	978-1-63676-478-8	*Paperback*
	978-1-63730-379-5	*Kindle Ebook*
	978-1-63730-380-1	*Ebook*

"The purpose of life is to discover your gift. The work of life is to develop it. The meaning of life is to give your gift away"

—DAVID VISCOTT

*To God for giving me a second chance and allowing me
to write this story and share it with the world.*

To life itself because every day is an adventure.

*To my parents and my sister for being there for me,
through the most intense moments of my life, and being a
fountain of love, compassion, and kindness for me.*

*To you, the reader, for believing in my story
and being part of my life journey.*

Thank you from the bottom of my heart.

Blessings to all.

CONTENTS

———

NOTE FROM THE AUTHOR

We all come into this world to live a life with a purpose. Every person is born with special talents and unique gifts that distinguish one person from another.

Help from Heaven is a true story about my near-death experience and how it gave me new life. In this book, I explain how I died and went to heaven, who I met there, and what happened there that changed me forever. It is a message of love, faith, and inner awakening.

I wrote this book because I felt an urgency to share my message with the world. I heard so many testimonials about how my story made an impact on other people, that I realized I do not want to die with this music inside my heart. I need to share it.

Many people have heard my story. They've contacted me and invited me to share my message. Over the last few years, I have shared my story in big churches, spiritual retreats, seminars, weddings, convention centers, hospitals, hospices, birthday parties, field trips, festivals, camping trips, podcasts, and social media.

After I gave my presentations in such a variety of places, it was clear to me my message influenced other people's lives, not just my own. In many cases, after I shared my message, people's reactions were overwhelming to me. I felt goose-bumps all over my body after seeing some cry and meeting some who just wanted to hug me. In some situations, people were shaking and jumping after hearing my story. I even met a woman who was so impressed after hearing my story she had an epileptic attack and I had to call 911. Paramedics arrived at the scene and calmed her down. When she was completely stabilized, she thanked me for telling her my tes-timony. Those were the biggest reasons I wanted to write this book. In the beginning, I did not know how I was going to do it, but I meditated and prayed about it and finally found the determination to share my story with as many people as I could.

Although these are my real-life stories, my message is not about me. It is about all of us—how we all came to this world to live a life with a purpose. My hope is you will love this book if you are trying to find your life purpose, looking for hope, or working to forgive people from your past.

The benefit of writing this book is to bring hope and clar-ity, even more so. is to bring self-help! I think this book will cause others to look for their own inner awakening. I want to give people a chance to remember their own experiences and see the possibilities in their own lives.

If it happened to me it could happen to you. You never know.

With all my heart,

Carlos Vivas

PART 1

BACK TO LIFE

CHAPTER 1

SHARING MY STORY

———

Sometimes we get involved in the same routine every day and we don't appreciate the beauty of nature around us. We don't stop to look at the trees, the birds, or the sky. One day in June 2020, I left work around 5:00 p.m. and as I walked to my car in the company parking lot I observed everything around me. The weather was a perfect eighty degrees with blue skies. It was a beautiful sunny day with a calm breeze that touched my face. I felt the need to get home, change my clothes, and go for a walk in the mountains near my house.

Feeling tired though, once I got home, I wasn't sure about going. I thought to myself, *you know what Carlos, let me look out the window one more time and see if it is worth it to go exercise my legs.* So, I looked out the window and it was sunny and beautiful outside and I decided I needed to go. However, as I was getting ready, I heard my inner voice say again, *Carlos, you're very tired. You shouldn't go hike a mountain or go for a walk. What you should do is take a shower and go to sleep. You have been working a lot lately and you need rest.*

I felt like a kid who wanted to disobey his parents. I thought, *wait. What?*

I said to my inner voice, *but look, there are blue skies and it's nice and sunny and warm outside.*

My inner voice said, *no. You're going to bed early today and that's it!*

I realized my inner voice was right. My spirit wanted to go for a walk and climb the mountains and enjoy nature, but my body was saying I needed rest. So, that's what I did. I took a shower. I got something light to eat and then I went to bed.

After tossing and turning and wishing I was outside I finally started to doze off when I heard a loud notification on my cell phone. I grabbed my phone, turned on the screen, and started checking the notification messages. I had a message on Instagram.

In a new alert, I saw an old friend of mine was live on an Instagram program. His name is Juan Alfonso Baptista. He is a very famous Venezuelan Colombian actor with whom I used to work a long time ago when I was a TV producer in Venezuela. We remain good friends even though we haven't seen each other in over twenty years.

I started watching his live program and saw him apologize to his audience.

He said, "Well, oh my God, I'm so sorry to everybody that is watching the program now. I know that this is disappointing and I feel very disillusioned about what just happened. This never happened to me before. I promoted this special program for about two or three weeks, but my guest, the actress scheduled for today, never showed up—no call, no show, not even a message saying she could not participate in my program. I don't know what happened. I was calling her. She never answered the phone. I have been doing this program for a long time and people show up and we always have a good time."

As I watched him, I felt sorry for him, because I know he is very respectful with his job and with all his guests, and this was a live program. He said he always has the actors, actresses, and singers come to the studio an hour before the program starts just to check the audio and answer any questions the guest has. But that day he didn't have any signs of the person he invited. She was a very famous actress in telenovelas (Spanish soap operas). He was really apologizing and saying he would have to improvise.

Juan said, "Well, everyone. I have a two-hour program. Let's see what we can do."

At this point, I was on the other side of the world in my room in Atlanta, watching him, and I thought, *let me send a message to say hello and give him some warm words of encouragement that everything will be fine.* So, I sent a message to him through Instagram messages, all of which he received were displayed on his screen so everybody could see them.

Then, he said, "Hey, I can't believe it. An old friend of mine just sent me a message on the live chat. Oh my God, he's watching my program! What a surprise! Hey Carlos, how you been doing brother? Long time no see."

"Hey Juan, I'm doing good, and you?" I replied.

"Hey, Carlos. I've been doing good. Thank you for asking. Hey, I have a question for you... now, here... live on air, what if you become my personality for the day and I interview you?"

At this point, he introduced me to everybody watching his program, explaining we are good friends even if we go a long time without talking to each other. He said he would love to interview me and tell everybody about my life story. After all, this interview program was about that—getting to know people and learn about the lessons they learned in life.

I was totally surprised and I wasn't prepared for this. It came out of the blue.

"Wait. What? Are you crazy, my friend?" I laughed. "My life is not that interesting. I don't know if people will like my story. I'm not ready or prepared for this. Actually, I was ready to go to sleep."

I laughed again, in a nervous way, and then I said, "Thank you for the opportunity, my friend, but I don't think so."

Then he replied, "Come on, Carlos. Let me interview you, please. Please, my friend."

Then I took a deep breath and said, "Well... okay. I'm in bed now, but let me put on a shirt and get ready."

A few minutes later I sent a message to him saying I was ready to broadcast. He could share the screen now. He divided his screen in two and just like that I was live on the air with him.

He welcomed me to his program and introduced me again to the public watching. He said, "Good afternoon ladies and gentlemen. Welcome to my program. This is my friend Carlos, everybody."

He went on to describe how we used to work together and he started telling the story of when I was a television producer and how successful our program was, twenty years ago. Then the interview started. I was feeling very comfortable because the way he conducted the program was very friendly. I didn't feel like I was in an interview at all. I felt like I was with an old friend, having a conversation about life and everything that happened to me in all the years since we'd last seen each other. Everything was going very smoothly.

"Hey, Carlos. How long have you been living in Atlanta, now?" he asked.

"Well, my friend, for about twenty years now."

"Wow, that's a long time, brother, and tell me about your work."

"Well," I said, "You know I care for people. I earned my certification to work in assisted living and my first job used to be working as a PCA (Personal Care Assistant) for elderly people who need help in their homes. I think it was the best job of my life because you feel the love that the patients give to you and vice versa. In this job, I met amazing people in their golden years and I just listened to their amazing stories about their life journeys. It was just awesome."

"It is a gift," I continued, "to hear those stories. Most of the time, I felt on that job like the only person they had in the world was me. Families just leave their elders there and the majority of the families—I will not say all the families—don't visit them often and my patients were very sad. I could lift their spirits by talking to them, by taking them on a walk in a park, or just by being a good listener. You know that's all that it takes; just be there for them. That's all that they need, to hear and feel they are loved by somebody. At that age, they feel like kids again—kids that need our attention, care, and support. It helps them feel better and more important if somebody cares for them."

"Now I work as a quality assurance manager for a service industry company, over sixteen years now. I like the job, you know; it pays the bills," I said.

"What else have you been doing all these years in Atlanta, brother? For example, what are you doing in your free time?" he asked.

"Well, in my free time, I've been doing some obstacle course racing. They are called Spartan races and they are obstacle races that you can do solo or with a group, but the fun is to go with a group, like for example, a fitness group or a bootcamp. I used to go with a group with ten people. And then you train for this. For example, for my first race, my bootcamp trainer, Tyler Moore, trained me and my group everyday five times a week, one hour a day for about five months to be in good shape to run better and overcome all the obstacles at a faster time."

"On the race day," I continued, "you go with your team. And you will have thirty obstacles to cross. You can help each other pass the obstacles if one of your teammates can't do it alone, crossing the obstacles faster and working as a team to finish in a decent time."

Juan Alfonso said, "Oh wow. I like teamwork. Helping one another to overcome all obstacles. And, I guess you enjoy all that adrenaline in that race?"

"Oh my God, yes! I love that!" I said.

"Okay, what else have you been doing, Carlos?"

"Well, I'm writing a book now," I said.

"Oh really? That's awesome. What kind of book are you writing, Carlos? I want to let you know that I interview authors on my program too, so it is a nice surprise for me, that you are becoming an author, too. So, tell me, what is your book about?"

"Well, my book is about a near-death experience that I had five years ago," I said.

With his mouth open and a surprised look on his face, Juan Alfonso said, "Oh my God, Carlos. You had a near-death experience? What happened to you? When did this happen? Thank God you are fine and here with us to share with us a bit about your story. It would be amazing if you tell us what happened to you."

I said, "Look, my friend, my story is a little long if you want me to go deep and share everything. I don't want to take too much time on your live program. We already talked for a while and I don't know how much time you have on air."

"Oh, don't worry, Carlos," he said. "We have over two hours left of our broadcast, so you can relax and take your time."

"Ok, well, here we go," I said as I started to describe my near-death experience.

I talked for about an hour and, in the middle of my story, Juan started getting emotional and I saw tears in his eyes.

"Oh my God, Carlos. Your story touched my heart. What a beautiful story," he said. "I'm amazed, Carlos. All of this came along out of the blue. Look what happened. Look at the way life played us here. The actress scheduled here today never showed up. She never called to cancel. It's like she disappeared. This has never happened on my program before and then you arrived on my program, without being planned, through a message on my Instagram and this just happened."

He continued, "You know, we, as humans, think we have it all under control and we think we have it all planned in our lives. Then, life happens and these amazing events take place without us planning it, Carlos. Do you know I planned this program for a long time, promoting it so enough people would be online today watching this special program, about this actress, but life said, 'Wait a minute. No. Let me change the circumstances and the guest.' This message is more important to air, because people need to hear your message about, love, life, purpose, and forgiveness."

He added, "Did you know that this platform is open worldwide and that people from all over the world were watching and heard your story? I started receiving messages from everywhere—people watching from all over South America, Europe, the United States, and other countries. All these people were waiting for the actress. And guess what? Life replaced her and put you in her place so people everywhere could hear your story. That is awesome!"

The show ended at about 9:30 p.m. and Juan said he would call me after it ended so he could personally thank me for being a guest. However, Juan didn't call me until almost 1:00 a.m.

"Hey Carlos," he said. "I'm very thankful that you wrote me a message and I could interview you on my program. Look, everything turned out great! Your story, believe me, is going to make an impact and it's going to help a lot of people."

I said, "Well, yes. I hope my story can move some people's hearts; you know."

"Carlos," he said. "You have a gift."

I said, "I have a gift? What are you talking about?"

He said, "Yes. You have the gift for the word. When you were talking, everybody was silent. They were just listening to your story. What an interesting story you have, you know, and everybody was paying attention and basically hypnotized by what you were saying."

"And the second thing that I want to tell you," he added, "after you hung up the phone, guess what? And this doesn't happen very often, Carlos. After I have an interview with an actor, actress, or singer and the interview ends, all the people on social media just drop the call. Guess what happened when you hung up? Everyone remained online for another hour because they wanted to know more about your story. So, let me tell you something, my friend. You need to spread the word. This message is not for you. This message is for humanity. This message is for people who need to hear it. People need hope in their lives and in their creator. So, please share your story, because it's a wonderful story."

This, my friends, is my story.

CHAPTER 2

DIAGNOSIS

My story begins when I was fourteen years old, a normal teenager attending a Catholic high school in Venezuela. I was a skinny guy, enjoying life. A normal day in my life was just going to school from 7:00 a.m. to 1:00 p.m. Typically, I enjoyed a long walk home, do my homework, and after that go to swimming and Taekwondo classes. Then, when I finished my classes, I would go home, take a shower, get dinner, watch some television, and go to bed around 9:00 p.m. or 10:00 p.m. That was my daily routine.

One day, on my way to school I got very tired and I didn't know why. I didn't pay attention, at that moment, to what was happening to me, but day after day I found myself debilitated. I didn't want to say anything to my parents because I didn't want them to worry about me.

By that time, my parents had separated and divorce. There was enough tension as it was. I was living with my mom then. She was very strict with me. I had to get good grades for her all the time and she never let me miss a school day. She wanted me to have perfect attendance. She would even go to my school to check on my grades! She was always talking with everyone in my school from the principal to my teachers about how I was doing. This was embarrassing to me.

All my friends used to tell me, "Dude, your mom is always coming to school to check on you. Wow, that puts a lot of pressure on you."

I used to think, well, that's the way she operates. I couldn't do anything to avoid the way she was.

Because my mom was so strict, I continued to feel bad for about a month without saying anything to her. I preferred remaining quiet so I just sucked it up. Then, one morning, while I was waiting at the bus stop to go to school, I had a blackout, meaning I faded out a bit and almost passed out. Somehow I was able to stand up again, but at that moment I knew I had to say something to my mom. That day after school, I went home and waited for my mom to come home from work. I was super scared to talk to her because I knew her. She was a single mother and she had enough on her plate raising me, and I knew she wanted the best for me. I thought she would think I didn't want to go to school. And that day, all day long, I rehearsed what I was going to say to her and the way I would deliver my message. I wanted her to understand what was happening to me and help me.

Finally, after waiting anxiously all day for this moment, she came home, tired after a long day at work. When I saw her I took a deep breath.

I counted in my mind, "five, four, three, two, one," and said, "Mom, we need to talk. Please. I know you will get busy making dinner, but believe me, I don't feel good."

"What's going on?" she asked.

"Well," I explained, "I have been feeling dizzy for weeks. I was hoping that the symptoms would disappear in a few days, but that was not the case. I still feel really low energy in my body and I think it's time to go to a doctor for a checkup to see what's going on with me."

She tilted her head to see if she believed me. Then she said, "That's fine. Let's go to the doctor."

Long story short, we visited over ten doctors, but none of them knew what I had. The last three doctors recommended my parents take me to see a specialist, specifically a hematologist, a doctor who specializes in blood. For my parents, that was the last option because he was the most expensive doctor in the city and I didn't have insurance at that time. In the end, we didn't have any other choice but to go see that doctor.

When we went to visit this doctor for the first time, I felt anxious and my leg was shaking as I waited to hear what he had to say about my symptoms. We got there at noon. As soon as we entered his office, the number of diplomas from all over the world impressed us. Can you imagine three office rooms full of diplomas and recognitions from so many countries? As we looked at and read these diplomas we could tell he was very famous, and, more importantly, knowledgeable in his field.

We waited for the doctor for about an hour before he arrived at his office. He was around sixty-five years old, six feet tall, with white hair and a lot of wrinkles. He was very polite and friendly. He finally asked me to step into his exam room so he could take my blood pressure and do a regular checkup of all my vital signs. After he finished, he told me he would analyze a series of blood tests and try to determine what was happening with me. He had a laboratory in another room next to his office where his wife was the doctor in charge. He took blood samples from my thumb and he went to the laboratory. I went back to the waiting area to sit with my parents.

Minutes later, he came back with the results and said they did not convince him of any particular illness.

"I can't believe this," he said and added that he needed to take another blood sample, this time from my arm.

I went back into the office. He drew the blood and left. I returned again to wait with my parents.

This time when the doctor returned he said, "I'm sorry, but that sample didn't convince me either. You are too young for this. Let me take a final blood sample, but, this time, from your back. Come back into my office and take your T-shirt off."

After a few minutes, he came into the exam room with a nurse. They told me to turn around, relax, and that they would start the procedure by taking a blood sample from my back.

I laid on the little bed at the doctor's office, facing the wall, and I felt the doctor rubbing a cotton ball with alcohol on a big area of my back.

Then, he said, "Relax, everything will be all right. Just take a deep breath and after that just breathe slowly please."

After that I felt them inject five shots of something into my back; I didn't know what it was or why he was doing this. It turned out it was anesthesia! I didn't know it at the time, but he had already spoken with my parents, who agreed and signed off on all the required paperwork for the procedure. Thank God I didn't know what he was doing. If I knew, I would have been super nervous, and maybe run out of the doctor's office.

As he gave me the shots, the doctor spoke again and said, "Please don't move. Just relax. This will be quick. Okay? The medication I just administered to you will start working. I need at least fifteen to twenty minutes for the medication to take effect, so please stay on this bed and wait. I will be back in twenty minutes."

Finally, after twenty minutes passed, I heard the doctor walking into the room with the nurse.

He said, "We are back. This is the last test. Please calm down and don't move, okay? Everything will be all right."

Then, I heard a drill! It was a microscopic drill like the ones used by dentists. I was laying on my side, facing the wall. I couldn't see what he was doing. I heard the drill start carving into my lower back as the doctor drilled something on my backbone. It was so noisy, but luckily I didn't feel much of anything because of the anesthesia. It just felt like a cork being pulled from a bottle of wine. It was a lot like that as I found out later he took a sample of something from my lower back.

My parents knew about the drill, but no one had told me. The doctor explained afterwards, if I knew about it, I would be more likely to move and I could end up a paraplegic if something went wrong. So, no one told me.

Then the doctor said, "Okay, I'm finished. It just took five minutes to perform this little procedure."

He rubbed my lower back with alcohol again and put on a bandage.

He said, "Okay, you can stand up and go to the lobby area with your parents until I call you guys to hear the results of the test. I'm going to the laboratory to run the analysis and when I finish, I will call you, okay?"

We waited anxiously for the results. About forty minutes had passed before a nurse finally said, "Okay guys, the doctor is ready to talk to you and give you the results of the analysis."

My mom, dad, and I stepped into the doctor's office. My parents sat down in front of the doctor's desk and I stood behind them. We waited about five minutes and then the doctor knocked on the door. He entered his office carrying a crystal glass with what looked like a cleaning solution in it and a red material floating inside.

He sat down and said, "Well guys, I got the results and this crystal glass has the sample of Carlos' bone marrow. I'm sorry to tell you guys, but I don't have good news. I practiced a series of blood tests on your son to see if I was wrong, but the last test shows the bone marrow speaks for itself."

There was silence in the room and everybody looked at each other.

Then, the doctor looked at me and said, "I'm sorry Carlos, but you have just three months."

I responded, "Three months? Three months for what?"

He replied, "Three months to live. You have a terminal illness and you waited too long to come in and get checked. The illness is too advanced in your body. I'm sorry; if you came in on time, it would have been treatable, but you came too late. Now, it's a terminal illness called leukemia."

As you can imagine, there was a lot of tension in that room, as my parents started crying inconsolably. I stood in the back, just watching this scene like a horror movie. I felt terrible because I didn't want to cause this pain to my parents, and I was trying to digest the bad news the doctor just gave us.

I also was mad—very mad. I wondered why this was happening to me. I was a good person. I kept trying to sort this out in my mind. I was in shock. I felt frozen.

The only words I heard from the doctor were, "I'm sorry. I'm sorry. There is nothing else to do."

Then I heard a whisper in my right ear. It was a very soft voice that said to me, "He doesn't have the last word. I have it. Do not worry."

I looked around to see who said that. I thought it was my imagination. All of a sudden, I felt like somebody injected me with valium. Peace came over my body. For the first time, I knew in my heart I heard the voice of God. I saw everything in slow motion. I felt calm, but I also felt excited. I knew everything was going to be fine. The peace was the confirmation I needed.

I started crying because I was so mad and I confronted the doctor. I pointed at the doctor's face and said, "Excuse me, doctor, but no. I'm not going to die in three months. No, no, no, and absolutely no."

My mom looked at me. Then, she looked straight at the doctor's face, and said, "Doctor, you are going to save my son's life."

The doctor replied, "I'm sorry, but that is not possible."

My mom stood up, leaned over the desk, grabbed the doctor by his V-neck shirt, and said, "Look me in my eyes and tell me that you have traveled all over the world to study this kind of sickness. You know there is something that can save my son!"

The doctor leaned back and said, "I'm sorry ma'am, but there's nothing else we can do to save your son's life."

My mom said, "Doctor, look into my eyes and tell me the truth. You just don't want to tell me, right? I know, doctor, you have sons and daughters and I know you would do everything in this world to save your own son's life. You would go to the end of the world to find a cure, right? Well, look at me then and tell me we can save my son's life."

The doctor looked at my mom, dad, and me, and after few seconds of silence, the doctor said, "Okay, I have two options, but I cannot promise anything, okay? Please sit down and I can explain them to you."

My mom let go of his shirt, looked at my dad, looked back at the doctor, and said, "Okay, I'm ready to hear how you can help us."

The doctor explained, "The first option is to travel to Houston, Texas, and do a bone marrow transplant. That way we can take the dying bone marrow and transplant some good and healthy bone marrow from an organ donor. As soon as the bone marrow starts working in your son's system, the white cell count will start increasing in his body and he could be healthy again."

"Okay, but doctor, how much will that surgery cost?" my mom asked.

The doctor said, "Well, it's very expensive. You may have to sell your house, your cars, and everything you own to cover the costs of this surgery. Remember, we need to find the organ donor first. Then you pay for the airline tickets, hotel, my accommodations, plus your family's accommodations for all the weeks we need to stay in Houston. This includes paying for the organ donor's expenses, the hospital expenses, plus the surgery. It will be a lot of money."

My mom looked at the ceiling, took a deep breath, and said, "Okay, doctor, if I sell my house, my cars, and all that I have, what are the chances that you can save my son's life?"

The doctor said, "It's a fifty-fifty chance. We don't know how his body will react when we transplant the new marrow. It could be that it will take it or it can refuse the bone marrow. There are no guarantees that we can save your son's life with this surgery."

Then, my mom looked at him and said, "Okay, so what you are telling me is that I need to sell everything I have and become homeless. And I will do that. But, you are saying to me that you can't promise me anything—meaning my son can die during the surgery, or right after the surgery. Is that right?"

The doctor said, "Yes, ma'am. That's a possibility."

Then, my mom replied, "Okay. I definitely don't like that option."

She took another deep breath and asked, "What is the second option?"

The doctor said, "Well, the second option is to travel to Europe, specifically to Paris, France, and go to a laboratory where there is a formula on which I am working with another doctor to help stop this disease. This formula, when taken along with vitamin C, can impact the bone marrow and maybe make it work again, thereby making it start producing white cells. It is basically synthetic masculine growth hormones. Maybe it will work. If we try that on your son, he will be a trial case. If you agree with that, then we can start with all the paperwork. You will need to fly to France and bring the medicine back here to Venezuela for the treatment."

He then added, "Do you want the transplant or do you want your son to be a guinea pig? At least you will be doing something, but you will need to sign a lot of paperwork to release me from any inconvenience caused by these two options."

My mom said, "I want to do something. He's not going to die because I didn't do anything. So, let's try the formula treatment."

We left the doctor's office in a daze.

At that time, my mom was working for the National Air Force of Venezuela. She spoke with one of her supervisors and told him about the experimental treatment. The captain of the air force told her, "Don't worry. I have to go to France anyway. I will bring the medicine back, but I need the permission and the money to buy the medicine and I will be glad to help you." So, he did.

It took a good month for the medicine to arrive. During that time, the doctor gave me a treatment with vitamin C and a cocktail of medicines mixed in an IV bag connected to a vein in my arm.

After weeks of waiting, it finally arrived. We went back to the doctor's office, so he could explain the dosage and how to use the formula. I was to take one pill a day with the cocktail of medicines I'd been taking. He warned me to prepare for many possible side effects like dizziness, loss of appetite, general discomfort, acne, and about twenty more symptoms. We accepted the challenge and I started taking the formula. For the next month and a half, I went to the doctor every week to get some blood samples to check if the formula was working.

Week after week, we went to the laboratory to get my blood tested and have a checkup. After a month of treatment, nothing happened. The level of the white cell counts continued to decrease. After every visit, my mom came home and started crying. I felt terrible because I didn't want to see her cry. I didn't like the fact that nothing worked and we couldn't do anything to make it work.

After a month and a half of the treatment, with no good news at all, I started thinking to myself, "There should be another way for me to get better."

I start thinking and thinking. Out of the blue, it came to my mind. I had an uncle who had a real estate company and he was the most wealthy family member I knew. When my mom came home from work that night, I told her I had an idea.

I said, "Mom, why we don't ask Uncle Cesar if we can borrow the money for me to have the surgery in Houston? We can work to repay him for the rest of our lives."

"Well," my mom said to me, "Please don't even try. You don't know him."

I said, "Mom, but he can help us! Please, mom!"

She said, "I'm sorry but that is not even an option."

That night, while I lay in bed, I could not believe what my mom told me. It made me so sad.

The next morning, after my mom went to work, I was alone at home when I thought, "Wait a second, the only person that is going to die is me. I need to do everything on my own to save myself."

I decided to call my uncle. I had a lot of hope and faith, believing he would help me. With happiness in my heart, I took a breath of hope and dialed my uncle's number. The telephone rang several times until he picked up the phone. I said hello to him and asked about my aunt and my cousins.

After he said everyone was fine, I said to him, "Uncle, I'm calling you because I need a huge favor from you and I cannot think of anybody else that can do me this favor, but you."

My uncle said, "Okay, Carlos, how can I help you?"

I told him the story about my terminal disease and how the only way I could survive was by traveling to Houston, Texas, for a bone marrow transplant.

I continued by saying, "So, I thought you could lend us the money to cover all the expenses of the surgery. Don't worry uncle, my mom, my dad and I will work all of our lives to pay you back for all the money you will loan us. You have to trust us."

With excited anticipation, I thought he would say, "Don't worry, I will help you." However, things did not turn out as I expected.

He took a deep breath and said, "I'm sorry, Carlos, but I can't help you."

Then, he hung up the phone.

As soon as he said that to me, I was petrified. I couldn't believe he had the heart to do that. At that moment, I dropped to my knees. I started crying and praying to God.

I said, "God, please help me. I don't have anybody else to turn to for help, but you. Please, God. Heal me from this disease. Only you can make a miracle in my life. Only you have the power to heal the sick. Only you know in my heart that I want to live to help people. Please give me another chance, another opportunity to live. From the bottom of my heart, God. I ask you for help. God, please, can you hear me?"

While I prayed and cried and asked God for help, I felt goosebumps all over my body and after that a heat that warmed my whole body and especially my heart. I knew something was happening at that moment. I didn't know what was going on, but it was a sign. I began feeling hopeful again and a sensation of wellness came over me. From that day on, I started praying constantly and declaring to God I was already healed. There was no doubt in my heart God was healing me.

I thanked God for my rapid recover and visualized myself walking outside in the park in perfect health, enjoying myself walking on a sunny day, enjoying nature, and giving thanks to God because I was already healed. I started thinking about the future and all the things I wanted to do when I grew up. I started feeling better and better every single day. Three months passed by. I was completing the treatment, and, after all my prayers, it was time for the doctor to run all the tests on me to check out how my body was responding to the treatment. They ran tests. I had CT scans and MRI scans.

On the day the doctor called us into his office to give us the results, my mom, dad, and I were so hopeful they would be different this time. As soon as we entered the doctor's office, he told us to take a seat. He had the results in an envelope. As soon as we sat down, he opened the envelope and started reading the results of all the tests. The final result was that I was completely cured. There was no trace of the illness anywhere in my body. I was free of leukemia.

At this point, my parent's faces illuminated with happiness and they told the doctor that because of those results, there was no doubt we were looking at a miracle!

My mom was saying, "Thank you, God. This is a miracle!"

Yet, the doctor's face was completely serious without a trace of emotion. Actually, his face was a sad face.

My mom asked the doctor, "But doctor, this is a miracle. What's the matter?"

He said, "I'm sorry ma'am, but we cannot use that word in our medical field for science. There is no such thing as a miracle. Unfortunately, I have more news for you. Your son was under a very intense treatment that chemically altered all the cells in his body and in his immune system in a way that he healed very fast, but, when we have had these cases of rapid recovery it's just momentary. It's called remission. This means the sickness disappears, but, in our experience, it has shown us that in these cases the illness comes back stronger. In most cases, it comes back worse than the first time, making it impossible to help the patient."

My mom started crying and said, "But doctor, it is a miracle; God saved my son."

The doctor responded, "Okay ma'am, time will tell us that I am right."

At that moment I stood behind my parents, listening to the diagnosis and watching the faces of my mom, dad, and the doctor. I couldn't believe what the doctor said.

I was completely in shock, until I thought to myself, "No, this is what he says. I completely refuse his interpretation. I declare I'm completely healed."

I had goosebumps all over and a heat overcame my body. Then, I heard a whisper in my ear that said, "No. He is wrong. This never will happen to you again."

I felt my heart warming and I knew inside of me, God performed a miracle in my life and I would never suffer from this illness again. That was it for me. From that moment on, I have always felt healthy, thanks to God, and from that day on I was grateful for the miracle he performed in my life.

CHAPTER 3

BOAT RIDE

On a Saturday afternoon in May 2015, I sat on the couch in my living room in Atlanta, watching the news. I was looking at all the craziness around the world, with so many stories about how bad the world was becoming. I didn't want to ruin my day with all of those bad stories, so I turned the TV off. I sat down, got comfortable on my couch, and looked out my window. The day was beautiful, and, for some reason, I started asking existential questions; I guess every person asks at least once in a lifetime.

I don't know if it was the news, or what was going on with me, but I suddenly had some questions for God. Not that I was doubting Him, but I started asking, "God, if you are real, if you really exist, answer these questions for me. Why are there so many people suffering around the world? Why are all these natural disasters happening—earthquakes, tsunamis, tornadoes, and all kinds of natural phenomena? Why are so many beautiful, innocent people dying? Why? God, why? Why is there so much hate between human beings? Why are there so many illnesses, terminal and not curable? Why does cancer affect so many people all around the world? There has to be an answer to my prayers. Please God, if you are out there, if you can hear me at this moment, I want to understand what's going on with humanity."

I stared out my living room window at the patio and garden. I saw the green grass outside, sunny skies, beautiful pine trees, birds flying around, flowers everywhere, and just a pure beautiful day. I was just thinking about how life can be more enjoyable, by just enjoying the little things we have in front of us.

As I looked out my window, I heard my cell phone ringing in the kitchen. I ran to answer the phone. It was one of my best friends, George, who is like a brother to me. His family almost adopted me as their son when I arrived in Atlanta over twenty years ago. They have always been so nice to me and a very lovely family. George called to see how I was doing, and he asked me if I had any plans for Memorial Day, which was around the corner.

"Well, you know what my friend? I really don't have anything planned. Do you have anything in mind?

He said, "Yes, I have a plan. What if we go to Florida to enjoy the weather and the beach? You go all the time, so you know the area better. We can find a good spot to stay for the weekend. My family is coming from out of town, and I would love to bring them, plus another friend, Enrique, with me.

I said, "Okay, let's do it then! Let me start looking for accommodations close to the beach and when we have everything together, we can meet and plan the trip better."

George said, "Okay! It sounds like a good plan.

The days passed and the weekend arrived. It was finally Friday and my friends, George and Enrique, George's parents, Nancy and Victor, were ready to go. We finally left Atlanta around 6:00 p.m. and with all the weekend traffic it took us forever to get out of the city.

Finally, after six hours of driving, we arrived at the hotel that night, tired after being on the road for so many hours. We checked in and got to sleep after midnight. The next morning, we all woke up around 7:00 a.m., tired, but excited. After everyone took showers and got dressed, we went downstairs to get our complimentary continental breakfast, which was very good. Everything was delicious.

After breakfast, we all were ready to go to the beach. The five of us got in the car. I drove because I knew the area. In the spring and summer, I went to the beach two weekends a month to relax from work and my daily routine.

We finally arrived at the first beach, but because it was a holiday, it was full. So, I drove to a second beach, and then a third one. They were also full.

I pulled over, looked at everyone and said, "Well guys, it looks like everyone came to the beach this holiday weekend, but don't worry. I have an idea. Let's go to a place not far away, a beautiful island on Panama City Beach called Shell Island. We can go to a marina and get a boat to drive us to the island. Most people don't know about this island, so I have a feeling it will not be as crowded as the regular public beach." They all agreed.

We drove to the first marina. I knew its location because I'd been there many times. When we pulled into the marina parking lot, I didn't see anybody. It was strange to see the marina empty. I told everyone to wait in the car while I checked the place out. I walked to the main office to see what was going on. The man at the front desk told me they were closed for renovations. I was very surprised because that marina was always open and full of people this time of year.

I came back to the car and I told everybody, "Hey guys, the marina is closed for renovations, but don't worry. I know another marina."

We drove to a second marina at the entrance to Panama City Beach. It was closed too! At that point, I didn't know any other marina. I started to feel as though something, or someone, was trying to tell me not to go. I kept trying anyway.

I looked at my cell phone and asked Google, "Hey Google, take me to another marina."

Google assistant responded, "You don't have permission to navigate on the internet now."

I looked at the phone screen and it was a blue background and some white letters, saying that I didn't have permission to navigate on the internet.

So, I got on my work phone which was on a different phone carrier.

I asked Google again, "Hey Google, take me to another marina."

Google said, "You don't have permission to navigate on the Internet."

That surprised me. Two different phones, with two different phone providers, but they both gave me the same message.

At that point, I asked my friends if someone could look it up with their phone.

They said, "Yes, sure, we will look it up."

They started to search online for another marina close to us and found out the only marina available early that morning was at St. Andrews State Park.

"Okay. Let's drive there," I said.

I was about to pull out onto the main street out of the parking lot, but there was one car approaching really fast on the lane close to me.

I thought to myself, "Should I go now or not?"

Something inside of me replied, "No. Let him pass him first and then you go."

Thank God I let the car pass. After he went by, I started to make a U-turn to go into the national park. As soon I did it, less than five seconds later, we heard a loud crash. It was the car I let pass. He crashed into two cars because he was driving so fast that he didn't see the traffic light. He went through the red light and caused an accident. I saw all this in my rear-view mirror. I was thankful I didn't jump into the street and instead let this guy in a hurry pass first.

We continued driving along the oceanside. The clouds were getting dark and we heard the rumble of thunder. Everybody looked at each other, George, Enrique, Nancy, Victor, and I, because the thunder was very loud. Seconds after that we saw lighting coming from the sky striking the ocean waters.

At that moment, George looked at me and said, "Hey, Carlos, don't you think we should go back to Atlanta? The weather is getting worse. Look at the clouds. Maybe a big thunderstorm is approaching and we are not going to enjoy the beach with this bad weather. Don't you think it will be better if we go back home?"

I looked at George and said, "Well, my friend, welcome to Florida! Here the weather is moody. It changes a lot. One hour it is sunny. The next hour it is cloudy and rainy, and then sunny again. It's okay. There is nothing to be afraid of; everything will be fine."

About fifteen minutes later, we arrived at the park. It was my first time coming here. There was a big line of cars to get in. We finally got to the security gate entrance.

We bought our tickets and were instructed to get on the shuttle bus to the marina where the boat would take us to Shell Island. We took the tickets and went back to the car to grab all the things we needed for that day at the beach. We thought the weather would eventually clear so we took our umbrellas, canopy, chairs, cooler, speakers, food, drinks, sunblock, and towels.

The shuttle buses were running at a scheduled time and our bus was leaving at 9:00 a.m. We walked to get in line to board the bus when George said, "Hey Carlos, I need to go to the bathroom. Do you think I have time to go?"

I said to him, "Yes, sure, but hurry up."

Ten minutes later the driver said, "Good morning everybody. Welcome to St. Andrew State Park. This is the shuttle bus that will take you to the marina. As soon as we arrive we will board the boat to Shell Island. Let's board the shuttle now, thank you!"

Everybody started boarding the bus. Most of the people were retired people living in Florida. The rest of the passengers were tourists from all over the US. As the bus began to fill up, I told the driver we needed to wait for my friend George. We waited fifteen minutes and he never showed up. I noticed the people on the bus were getting impatient, so I asked George's dad if he could go and see if something happened to his son. As he got close to the bathroom, he could hear George yelling, "Hello. Is anybody outside? Somebody just locked the bathroom door. Please, help me. Let me out of here. I need to catch my bus."

George's dad, in desperation, and nervous hearing his son trapped in that bathroom, yelled to his son, "Hey son, are you okay? This is your father. Don't worry. I will look for help. Let me go to the main office. I will be back soon. Calm down, please, everything will be fine. I will look for a way to get you out of there."

He ran to the office and found the manager at the main desk. He explained what happened. The manager said he didn't know how that happened. What a strange thing.

Once again, I felt a little voice inside telling me not to go. The sensation in my stomach felt like a sign something bad would happen if I went. I was nervous.

Finally, the janitor came with a master key and opened the door. George came out and hugged his father.

His father asked, "Are you okay?"

George replied, "Yes. I'm fine. Thank you."

"Thank the janitor. He was the hero who got you out of the bathroom, George. Thank him."

They laughed a little and George's dad said, "Okay. Hurry up. Let's run to the bus before we miss the ride."

They finally arrived at the bus and we took off.

Then the driver said, in a mysterious tone of voice, "Are you ready to go on an incredible adventure to the most famous island by the Gulf of Mexico, here in Panama City, where you will enjoy the most beautiful crystal waters in Florida and an amazing variety of sea life animals? If you are lucky enough you will be able to see and spot manatees, dolphins, or a stingray. Let's go to the marina and let the adventure begin."

Five minutes later we arrived at the marina. I looked through my bus window when we arrived. As I looked around at the green grass, blazing white sand, and the deep blue ocean, I realized how beautiful life is.

CHAPTER 4

BEFORE THE STORM

———

"May I have your attention please. May I have your attention, please?" said the bus driver.

"Okay guys, let me tell you the bus schedule. The boat to the island and the shuttle bus are connected, which means every hour from now until 5:30 p.m., a boat will go back and forth to Shell Island. So, make sure you are on time. I'm telling you it is not fun to miss the last boat and stay on the island until the next day. There is no electricity, no bathrooms, no shelter to stay in or spring water to drink—plus it's cold and windy. I wish everyone a fantastic Memorial Day at Shell Island. Enjoy your stay."

My friends and I started walking away from the bus. We picked up our chairs, towels, canopy, cooler, umbrellas, tubing, food, and water; afterwards, we walked to the marina ramp and a wooden deck, at the end of which was the boat waiting for us to board. As soon as we boarded the boat the driver said, "Welcome everyone. Sit down please." Then, after explaining the safety procedures to ride the boat, we sailed out into open water on the way to Shell Island.

The sky was blue and clear. The waters were kind of blue with turquoise color. The scenery was beautiful. I sat down next to an open window and the fresh breeze and salty water sparkled all over my face. It was a nice ride. About twenty-five minutes later, the boat started to approach Shell Island. The weather looked good with blue and sunny skies. The waters were crystal clear. It was a little piece of paradise off Florida's Gulf of Mexico, with emerald waters, pure white sands, and a beautiful piece of land in the middle of the ocean. There were a few palm trees and a little vegetation, but it was very hot. This was why we had to bring everything with us—so we would have shade throughout the day at this beach.

As we approached the bayside, I noticed a lot of families were on that side of the island enjoying the weather. So, I asked the boat driver if he could take us to the backside of the island, the side with open ocean waters.

He said, "This is the safer part of the park. If you want to go to the other side you will have to walk on your own that way, because I'm not going over there."

I said, "Okay. That's fine. I was just asking. Thank you!"

As soon we landed, I put my bare feet on the sand. It was a relaxing sensation that made me feel like I was finally on vacation. I started walking and led my group past the bayside natural pool, where many families were spending the day with their children. I thought the other side of the island, where the ocean was, would be a good place for us to camp because it wouldn't be too crowded. We dragged everything through the sand—all the chairs, umbrellas, coolers, and everything we brought. We had to walk along the beach between the families.

As I passed by a father watching five kids playing in the sand, he called to me and said, "Excuse me. Excuse me, sir. Where are you going with all those things? This is the end of the bayside area and all the families are here."

I responded, "Well sir, I'm going to the other side of the island."

He responded, "Oh, please don't go that way. Stay on this side, where all the families are."

I asked him, "Sir, why don't you want me to go that way?"

He said, "This side is safer, plus, it is very windy on the other side now. The waves are huge and the ocean is dangerous today."

I said, with a confident voice, "Sir, don't worry. I've been coming to this island for years and nothing bad ever happens. Plus, I have been on a swimming team for several years. I'm a good swimmer, but thank you for your advice. We will try to be careful. Don't worry. We will be fine. Thank you for your concern."

As I said this to the man, I continued walking to the other side of the island with my friends. After ten to fifteen minutes, we arrived on the other side. There was nobody there but us. I thought it was because the ocean was rough, with its big waves and the heavy wind. We continued walking, looking for a good camping place. We finally found a good spot and unpacked all our stuff, including the chairs, the cooler, the speaker, the floaters, the surfboards, and food. To complete the camp, I brought a big blue canopy, big enough to accommodate ten people. I started opening the canopy with my friends and at that moment the wind started blowing really hard. The canopy opened like a parachute and there was no way to ground the canopy. We tried for over an hour, but the weather wasn't helping.

After many attempts to settle down the canopy, it was still flying away with the heavy winds. My friend's father, Victor, said, "Hey guys, why you don't go and get some rocks from that little hill."

George and I thought that was a great idea. So, we went to the hill and gathered some rocks to put in a pile at each post of the canopy. That was the only way the tent would stay put. Now the canopy was set up, strong on the sand with the help of those rocks, and it was looking nice and firm.

George, Enrique, Nancy, Victor, and I set up our camp area for the day, with the chairs, food, drinks, and the rest of the equipment we brought. We spent the next few hours having a good time chilling in front of the beach. The time started passing by, fast, while we sat inside the canopy, playing games and telling stories. Around 3:00 p.m., I started to get tired and I fell asleep. An hour later, I woke up to everyone packing and getting ready to go.

It was now 4:00 p.m. and everyone in the group wanted to take a walk around the island before the last boat took off at 5:30 p.m. One of my friends asked me if I wanted to go with the group to walk around the island.

I said, "No. Thank you, but I will stay at the campsite and take care of everything. You guys can go and have fun. Don't worry about the camp. I will be fine here."

They left and about ten to fifteen minutes later, I started getting bored. It was very hot, sunny, and humid.

I said to myself, *it's too hot here. I'm going to have to refresh myself. I'm going to swim near the beach in front of the campsite for a bit and then I'll come right back.*

I ran into the refreshing water. Even though the weather was hot, the water was cold. You know, it takes a minute for your body temperature to get comfortable with the ocean water temperatures, so I started walking deeper and deeper into the ocean waters. Then, I started noticing there were holes in the sand as I was walking. I kept falling in these holes. It was a little strange to me. I never experienced these holes on this beach before. I thought it was something nature formed that day under the water, so I didn't pay too much attention and continued walking. Then, I started swimming for about fifteen minutes when I looked up and saw Enrique walking to the beach where I was swimming. He was coming back from the group by himself.

I yelled to him, "Hey, what's up? Why did you come back?"

He yelled, "I came back in case something happens to you. I don't want to leave you alone here."

I said, "It's okay. Don't worry, bro."

He got in the water and swam with me for about ten minutes.

Finally, he got out of the water and started walking away from the beach. He said, "Hey, the sun is very hot and it's burning my skin. I'm so white that I feel like a ghost. I need to put some sunscreen on if I don't want to fry like a shrimp from the sun. Let me go back to the campsite. I will be back."

I gave him a thumbs up and he left. I continued swimming for about another ten minutes.

After this time, I thought to myself, *okay. That's enough swimming. I'll go back to the tent with my friend.*

I started walking toward the beach and when the water was at my waistline, I noticed something weird. Every time I stepped toward the shore, I felt something pulling my legs back into the ocean. The water level started rising rapidly as if a giant was filling the ocean with water. As soon as the water came up around me it would cover me up. I jumped to get some air and as soon as I jumped, a strong current under the water pulled at me. It felt like a whirlpool and vacuum were pulling me back into the ocean.

CHAPTER 5

STORMY WATERS

———

A powerful current under the water started to push me into the ocean. I desperately tried to swim out, but the beach was hard to see because there were no breaking waves. The tides were rising and falling and I didn't know what was happening. Let me tell you something. I didn't know what a riptide was before, but I learned in the worst way possible. This one was very strong. It was a narrow current of water moving directly away from the shore, cutting through the lines of breaking waves like a river running out to the sea. It was strongest near the surface of the water.

If you get caught in a riptide and you do not understand what is going on or you do not have the necessary skills to escape, you may panic or exhaust yourself by trying to swim directly against the flow of water. So, guess what happened to me? I was one of those guys who didn't know what to do because I was in despair. I tried to fight against the current and go back to the beach. This current was so strong that in a matter of seconds it pulled me out into the ocean, far away from the shore.

Believe me, I swam for five years on a swim team when I was a child. I thought I knew how to swim in the ocean, but that was far from the truth. I was fighting against the current to get back, but it was impossible. I swam and swam and swam. Every time I lifted my head to see how close I was, I became farther away from the island. That made me fight even more until I started to realize I was losing hope. The current was taking me backwards. I still kept fighting for about twenty minutes. My legs had muscle cramps. I reached the point when I started to panic. I realized I was reaching the end of my life. The scenery was perfect. I was far out in the ocean. Big waves and freezing water surrounded me. No one was watching. The rip current was sucking me deeper into the ocean. It was taking all of my energy.

When I became aware of all of this, I thought to myself, *you know what? This is the end.*

With fear invading my entire body and all my thoughts, I had tears in my eyes. I knew there was no way I was going to get back to shore alive. Nobody was watching, so I had zero hope. This was it.

I thought to myself, *you know what, Carlos? Before I die I will do one more thing.*

I was completely in tears and could barely manage to stay afloat. Exhaustion set in, but when you are in a situation like this—when you are dying—your body produces a lot of energy because you don't want to die. So, I took a deep breath and I began to pray.

Thank you God, for everything you gave me in this life. I give thanks to you for my family. Thank you for my mom, my dad, my brothers and sisters, my friends, and everybody who walked next to me in my life. Thank you for everything you have given me. I really want to say thank you from the bottom of my heart. I'm sorry if I did something wrong. I think I did my best in my life, but I'm ready for you if you want to take me now, God.

During the agony of what I thought were my last moments, I heard a calm voice behind me whisper, "Ask for help."

"Excuse me… wait what?" I said, looking around.

I looked everywhere, but I didn't see anyone. Then, I heard it again.

"Ask for help," said the voice.

I thought, "Is this a joke? There is nobody watching. There is no hope!"

I heard the voice again. For the third time, it said, "I told you to ask for help."

I asked, "Who is behind me?"

Then, the wind started blowing by my ear and I just heard silence.

So, I said to myself, "Okay. Okay. Okay. Because this is the last thing I will do in my life, I will ask for help with all my heart. Even though I believe that nobody will hear me, at least I will know if I die that at least I did something. I will try to get saved."

Then, I started screaming, "Help! Help! Please help!"

After several minutes, I saw somebody on the top of a rock hill. Guess who it was? Yes, I rubbed my eyes. I couldn't believe it. With tears in my eyes and happy emotions in my heart, I saw it was one of my friends. It was Enrique.

I started screaming from the top of my lungs, "Enrique! Hey! Help me. Please! Hey!"

He was jumping and yelling at me, "Carlos, please hold on. I will get some help! I'm calling 911."

I saw him run as fast as he could towards the camp. A few minutes later, he was back at the top of the hill and carrying inflatable tubes and boogie boards. He yelled at me and started throwing the tubes and the boogie boards off the cliff, but the wind worked against him. Every time he threw a tube at me it flew back to him.

When he finally realized it wasn't working, he yelled at me again. "Hey Carlos, please hold on. I will be back. I will look for more help!" he said.

I was so far away, I barely heard what he said. He ran to the other side of the beach. Let me tell you, this island is a piece of land in the middle of the ocean and it's not that big. My friend ran to the bayside, the calm side with no waves where all the families were with their kids. He yelled for help and a lot of people from that side of the island started running to the ocean side of the island, where I was. They followed my friend up to the top of a hill where the view was clearer. Some guys also ran and started climbing up a rocky hill to see where I was in the ocean.

Everybody was yelling, "Please hold on. Please hold on!"

Six different men jumped from the top of the rocks into the deep and stormy waters to try to save me. Each person started swimming my way until they realized I was too far away to reach. The weather didn't help. It was very windy. The water was cold. The waves were big and the people who jumped in to rescue me started to realize there was no way they could rescue me under those circumstances. No one wanted to risk their lives to save me. One by one they turned around and right in front of my eyes I saw my hope vanish.

As I watched everyone swim back to the shore, I said to myself, "Okay. This is it. I'm done, but I will fight until the end. I'm not going to give up that fast." As soon I thought this, I saw a very short teenager swimming in my direction.

He yelled to me, "Hey, don't worry. I will get you out of here. I came to save you."

I thought, "Oh, Lord! God, have mercy. Look at this kid." I could see he was a small guy, whereas I am a big guy. I thought, "There is no way this guy is going to save me and take me out of here and save himself out of this mess."

I yelled to him, "Hey! It's okay. Please go back. You are too small. I'm a big guy and I don't want you to die with me, so please go back!"

He didn't listen to me. He yelled back, "No. I came to save you!"

I knew he couldn't make it out to where I was, so I yelled again, "Please go back. Please, listen to me. Go back!"

Suddenly, he realized he was in the riptide current too. He started yelling, "Oh no! I'm in it, too! It's sucking me into the ocean. I'm going to die. Oh no!"

I shouted, "Oh, my God. I told you to go back!"

Instead of trying to grab him, I started yelling at him. "Come on. You can get out of the rip current! Come on, man. You can do it! Come on. Come on! Swim away from the current."

Guess what? He did. Miraculously, he escaped and went back to the safety of the shore.

While all this was happening, I was still fighting the water, trying to stay afloat and not drown. After fighting so much, my legs and arms started cramping up. I felt a cold freezing sensation. I started shaking and I realized I was running out of time.

At that moment, I thought to myself, *okay, Carlos. This is really it. I'm coming to the end. I don't have enough energy to continue swimming and keep myself afloat.* At that moment, I felt helpless and hopeless. I thought, *well, the time has come to say goodbye.* I looked to heaven and said very loudly, "Please God, help me! I surrender to you!"

Suddenly, the waves became a little bit more aggressive. The water levels rose higher and the water felt colder and colder. I tried to stay afloat, but the cramps in my legs and arms started hurting too much at this point. It was hard to keep swimming. The waves were rising too high. They crashed over me, again and again, until a big, heavy wave came over me and pushed me all the way to the bottom of the ocean. I was spinning without direction and suddenly I blacked out.

The blackout only lasted what seemed like a few seconds. I opened my eyes and everything was silent except for the sound of water bubbles. At that point, I had suffered so much fighting with the riptide I didn't care anymore. Then, something started happening. I saw a big shadow going in circles around me. The shadow went under me and continued moving in a circle. All of a sudden, something pushed me up and out of the water. I couldn't believe what I saw. It was a big grey dolphin. I thought I was dreaming. He lifted me up from under the water and kept me afloat. It was an amazing moment I will never forget. My mouth was wide open. I was amazed at the sight. I stared into the dolphin's eyes and questioned myself.

How could this be possible? How did he hear me?

I didn't have any energy left. This dolphin came right on time. I looked straight into his eyes with a thankful expression and I grabbed him by the tail and held on for about ten minutes. At this point, everybody from the shore was screaming and watching. They saw everything that was happening.

Ten minutes later, a little fishing boat arrived. When he was fifteen feet away from me, the fisherman yelled, "Hey, I came to rescue you, but the ocean waves are very rough and the size of the waves are too big. I cannot get close to you, because I may hit you with my boat and knock you out. The only thing I can do is throw you a rope. As soon as you catch the rope, you can pull yourself towards the boat. Is that okay?"

I nodded, "Okay."

I grabbed the rope and started pulling myself toward the boat. When I got to the middle of the boat, I held the rope really tight and the pain from the cramps was kind of intense. I couldn't move because I was freezing and stiff.

The fisherman yelled to me one more time, "Hey! Hey! What are you doing? Don't just stay there! Come on. You need to get into the boat. Move to the back of the boat! There is a staircase in the water. Climb the stairs and come on board. We need to get out of here as soon as possible."

I told him I was freezing and I had cramps.

He replied that his boat was sinking.

I asked, "What do you mean it's sinking?"

He said, "I had a water pump on my boat, but all of a sudden it stopped working. The boat is getting flooded now. Hurry up and get in."

As soon I heard the desperation in his voice, I got the energy. I don't know from where, but I moved as fast I could to get inside the boat. I don't know how I did it, but I climbed up the stairs and flopped into the boat. As soon I got on board, I saw the boat was full of water, like a swimming pool. I looked at him with more fear.

He said, "Exactly. The boat is full of water."

As I was catching my breath, I asked, "Do you have a bucket to empty out the water?"

He said, "No. I don't. Could you please sit down? I will try to get us out of here as soon as possible."

He pointed to a seat on the boat. I sat down. My whole body was shaking.

He looked at me again and said, "Don't worry. You are saved."

CHAPTER 6

A LIGHT IN THE OCEAN

———

As we rode back toward the island, the fisherman began asking me questions, like what was my name and if I was fine after what happened to me on the beach. I explained to him I was just swimming on the shore when this strong current sucked me into the ocean where my battle with the rip currents started. I didn't know it was a deadly current. He explained to me those currents are frequent during certain times of the day along the shores and that I am never to swim alone again, even if I know how to swim.

While he talked to me, he looked out at the horizon. Then, he looked back behind the boat and said to me, with a surprised face, "Oh my God! You're not going to believe who is following us."

I asked, "Who?"

He started screaming at me, "Look behind you! Look behind you!"

Even though my body was stiff and still shaking, I stretched around to look back and I couldn't believe what I saw. It was the dolphin who saved me. He was following us, jumping behind the boat. The fisherman, impressed by the dolphin's act and knowing what a special moment this was, pulled out his cell phone and recorded a video of the dolphin.

Then, the fisherman said to me, "I will take you to a safe place all the way on the back of the island—the leeward side. It's calm there and the water level is at your knees. I will leave you there."

"Are you okay to walk?" he asked. "You will need to walk to where everybody is and it's not too far from where I will leave you."

"Yes. That's fine. I'm okay to walk. As soon as I touch the ground everything will be fine with me," I said.

He said, "I would go with you, but I need to repair my boat."

Finally, we got to the calm side of the island. I looked at the beach. Nobody was there, because they were still on the other side of the ocean where they'd gone to rescue me. This side of the island was empty—no people, no families. With my face full of tears and my grateful heart, I said goodbye to the man who saved my life. I thanked him for rescuing me from the ocean and the fisherman said to me, "God bless you!"

He helped me carefully get off the boat and waited for me to start walking to the shore.

Then, he yelled to me, "Are you okay? Can you make it to the shore?"

"Yes. I can," I said. I waved at him as he left and yelled, "Thank you!"

While I walked to the shore, I felt like something was following me and I felt something touch my right leg. I looked back and to my surprise, it was the dolphin who saved me. He was behind me. As soon I saw him, I exclaimed, "Oh my God!" I put my hands over my face and I started to cry. I couldn't believe it. It was the most magical moment. I was so grateful I was alive. I removed my hands from my face and began walking. He stayed right next to me as I continued to shore.

I finally reached the beach and dropped to my knees to pray.

I said, "Oh God. Father, thank you for saving my life. I need to tell you something that I feel and it's coming from the bottom of my heart at this moment. If you saved me with this dolphin, it is because you want something from me. I don't know what you want. Maybe you have a new purpose for my life. But, I'm telling you. Carlos just died in the ocean and the person who is walking out the ocean waters—well it's going to be you from this moment. I want you to come down to earth and take my soul, take over my body, get inside of me, and do whatever you want to do. Not tomorrow. Not later. I want you to take over now! I promise you from today forward, you will direct this new life."

As I was on my knees, I could hear thunder in the distance. The sky was getting dark as if a big storm was coming. I saw lightning around me and a delicate mist of rain start pouring down. The rainwater started sliding down my whole body. I didn't know at that time how much that promise would impact my life. I just cried like a baby, thinking I should be dead instead of safe at the shore. A dolphin, a fisherman, and God saved my life.

The only thing that crossed my mind was gratitude for every good person that came into my life—every friend and family member. My life flashed before my eyes in seconds. I was back, but now I wasn't going to waste time with little things. I pledged to spend more time with my family and friends. I wanted to enjoy every moment of my life from now on and I vowed to help as many people as I could. From now on, I wanted to inspire people. I wanted to make a difference in their lives and encourage them to be better parents, better brothers and sisters, better sons and daughters, and better neighbors. I wanted to share my love and kindness with the world.

At that moment, as I thought and reflected on my life, I completely surrendered to God. I knew that my life, after this encounter with the dolphin, now had a purpose. Whatever God wanted me to accomplish would be done. Several minutes after I said these words to God, people from the other side of the island came running to me to check how I was.

Everybody started asking me, "Are you okay? What happened?"

People I didn't know start hugging me and they cried, "Oh my God! Oh my God! You survived. You are alive!"

That's all I heard from everyone. I felt them hugging me and an immense feeling of protection and love enveloping me. I felt immensely happy in my heart for this new opportunity—for this new start.

People started asking me if I was fine and if I needed a doctor. I told everyone I was okay. I just wanted to go back to the office at the national park, St. Andrews State Park, and talk to the authorities. I wanted to tell them what happened to me and make sure they were aware and alert, as the same thing that just happened to me could happen to anyone on this island.

Finally, we took the boat back to the park and I went to the main office where I bought my ticket. I asked to speak to the managers of the park. I explained to them all that happened to me. They apologized for not having any lifesavers on that side of the island, but told me they would take care of it so this incident would not happen again. They were really nice and happy to see me alive and perfectly fine.

My friends and people who came from the beach with me walked from the park office to the parking lot. One of my friends asked me what I wanted to do next. I told him I really wanted to go to a church. I knew what happened to me was a miracle and I needed to give thanks to God.

I grabbed my cell phone and I started looking online for a Catholic church. Raised under the Catholic religion, I felt a strong desire to find one nearby. I asked Google assistant, "Hey Google. Take me to the closest Catholic church."

Google answered me, "The closest Catholic church near your location is St. Bernadette Catholic Church."

I said to my friends, "Let's go to that church."

I don't know how the time flew by, but when we got to St. Bernadette's it was already 9:00 p.m. We got out of the car and walked toward the door. To our surprise, we found it closed. We walked around the church and found a chapel in the middle of a garden. It was a type of cave. Inside this cave, at the far end, was a statue of the Virgin Mary of Fátima. Inside this chapel, there were over a dozen lit candles. Outside, there were three little statues representing the three children who saw the Virgin, early in the 1900s, when the story of Virgin Fátima began.

I said, "Everybody who came with me, I want to say thank you for following me and giving thanks to God for the miracle that we all witnessed. Now, it's time to pray and say thanks. Let's stay here in front of this little chapel. Since we can't all fit in there, let's make a circle and pray in the garden in front of the chapel."

That's what we did. We prayed for over twenty minutes, giving thanks to God for saving my life with the beautiful dolphin. After we finished the prayers, we all hugged each other. I thanked everyone for coming to the church and we went back to the parking lot. We all got in our cars and one by one everyone left and I drove our car back to the hotel.

As soon as we arrived at the hotel, I was hungry and tired. I grabbed something to eat, took a shower, and went to bed. It had been quite a day.

CHAPTER 7

UNEXPECTED DREAM

———

That day, the day of my near-death experience, my life changed forever. When I went to bed that night I thought the day was done and I would be able to rest. Little did I know, God still had a message for me. That night I had a dream. It wasn't a regular dream. It was a vivid dream in 3D with a response, a message, and a big meaning. In my dream, I opened my eyes and found myself on the third floor of a Caribbean cruise ship. I sat at a long dining room table with all my coworkers from my office. Everybody was eating lunch, having a good time, telling stories, and laughing. In front of me I was overlooking the ocean. It was about noon. The sun was right above the ship. I was looking at the blue ocean and I immediately realized something was wrong. I didn't know what it was. I started looking in all directions to see what was going on. I studied the horizon and could see something was approaching the ship from far away. I realized it was a big ocean wave coming toward us. It was a tsunami.

I looked out with horror on my face. I took a deep breath and in a loud but calm voice, I said, "Oh no. Look out there. Look at the ocean everybody. It's a tsunami and it's heading our way. There is nowhere to go. We are in the middle of the ocean."

Someone at the table asked me, "So what should we do?"

I said, "There is nothing we can do. We just wait to get hit by the huge wave. The only thing we can do is adopt the crash position and pray to God to save us. Cross your arms, protect your face, and wait for the impact."

At that moment, I started hearing people praying, others crying, and some asking, "Why us?" All we could do was wait, and wait, and wait. Ten, twenty, then thirty minutes passed by, but nothing was happening.

I then said to myself, "Okay. So what's going on? What's happening? Where is the tsunami? We were waiting for a long time and nothing?"

Then. somebody appeared. He was standing behind me and touching my upper arm. And He said, "Hey Carlos, wake up."

I said, "What? Wake up? No! I don't want to wake up."

He asked, "Why don't you want to wake up?"

I said, "Because, I died."

He repeated back to me, "Because, you died?"

I said, "Yes. I died."

He continued, "How did you die?"

I said, "Well, a tsunami came and killed everyone on this boat."

He said, "You didn't die Carlos. Come on. Open your eyes."

I said, "I'm not opening my eyes."

He asked, "Why Carlos?"

I said, "Because, I am dead."

He said, "You are not dead and you will never die with me."

I said, "What? Who is this?"

I was afraid but intrigued to see who was talking to me. At that point, I opened my eyes very slowly and looked behind me. All I could manage to see was a big man, around 6'5", dressed in a white robe. I couldn't see His entire face, only up to his chin. A white halo of light surrounded Him. I thought, "Is this Jesus?" and something inside of me said, "Yes, it's Him."

At that moment, He said, "Okay Carlos, close your eyes again."

He then grabbed me and hugged me from behind.

After a few seconds, He said, "Okay. Carlos, you can open your eyes now."

Even though I was afraid, I slowly opened my eyes. Surprised, I saw I was in the middle of what looked like a huge golf course with amazing green grass, blue skies, and thousands of people, all in front of Jesus and me. We stood at the top of a hill. All these people stood along the hill. Jesus stood behind me and I was in front of him.

The first words that came out of my mouth were, "Oh my God. I'm dead!"

Jesus said, "No. Carlos, you are not dead."

I said, "Okay, then why are these people dressed in white robes like you? This is all so beautiful and perfect. This is heaven."

His reply was, "Yes. It is heaven, Carlos. Calm down. Everything is fine. I just want to welcome you."

I said, "Welcome me? Welcome me to where?"

He replied, "welcome you to heaven and to our group, Carlos. From this moment on, you are part of me and part of my group. From this moment, you will start walking with me and walking with them. From this moment, you will be saving lives with me."

I said, "Saving lives? Who, me? I don't know how to save lives."

He said, "Don't worry. I will show you how. I want you to walk with me in heaven."

We started walking around while my eyes looked to the horizon and saw all the thousands of people, just standing there.

I said, "Jesus, I have a question."

He said, "Yes, Carlos."

I asked, "Where are all these thousands of people from?"

Jesus said, "They are from all over the world."

I asked, "What religions are they?"

Jesus said, "Carlos, in heaven, there are no religions. The only thing you will find in heaven is love. Love is the only thing you will find here. Did you know that love is the most powerful energy force in the universe and love is the force that will unite all humanity into one?"

At that moment a big sunset, with bright orange and yellow colors, appeared in the sky; Jesus looked up to the sky. He smiled and looked at me. Then, he hugged me and we continued talking until I woke up.

The dolphin incident and the dream happened over the weekend, Saturday to Sunday, during my stay at the hotel at Panama City Beach. I was so moved by these incidents and they were so fresh in my mind that I couldn't wait to go to work and tell my story to everyone on Monday.

I was so excited I was alive, rescued by a dolphin, and, as if that wasn't enough, I met Jesus. At about 7:30 a.m. on Monday, I was back at my office sharing my story with my coworkers. Much to my surprise, some of them started laughing.

I looked at everyone with a serious face and said, "You guys think I'm joking, right? You don't believe anything, but it's okay. I know what I saw. I know it was real. I felt it in every fiber of my soul and that's enough for me."

My boss walked into my office and said, "I was behind you and I had to stop to hear your story. I believe you, Carlos. Let me tell you, these guys are laughing because they don't believe in anything."

I asked, "What do you mean?"

He looked back at me and said, "Carlos, they are atheists. I am a Christian and I believe in God, but now I want you to go to your computer and Google how many times dolphins rescue and save people on the beaches and in the oceans all around the world."

I said, "Wait. What? Come on. I never heard that before."

He replied, "Go ahead. Search online."

I did. I sat down at my computer and started tapping the question in the search bar. The answers came right away. I found many cases reported around the world. Dolphins, these intelligent mammals, help humans get out of dangerous situations, not only when they are down, but also when sharks are nearby. These mammals protect the lives of humans in danger from the predator sharks. There were dozens of articles found in historical references from hundreds of years ago.

Then, my boss asked me to search how many people die by being caught in a riptide. I looked and according to the United States Lifesaving Association, riptides are the leading cause of rescues by lifeguards at beaches and they cause over one hundred deaths by drowning per year in the US.

Finally, he told me to look up how many dolphins die every year around the world at the hands of humans. According to the Animal Welfare Institute, more than 100,000 dolphins, small whales, and porpoises (small cetaceans) are slaughtered globally in hunts each year, many become fishing bait. That surprised me and I couldn't believe humans treat these beautiful mammals that way, knowing dolphins are so gentle with us. I knew that firsthand.

PART 2

SIGNS OF LIFE

CHAPTER 8

MY FIRST REVELATION

———

A few days passed by and on the Wednesday after my near-death experience, my boss sent me to a customer's house to fix a lamp. He said one of our employees broke it during a house cleaning. Our crew member moved a tall lamp in her basement and broke a piece off the lamp. My boss asked me if I thought I could fix it.

I said, "Sure, let me go and take a look."

I went to the house, located in the city of Stone Mountain near Atlanta, just thirty minutes away from my office. When I rang the bell, the customer came to the door. I introduced myself and she was glad I came so quickly.

She said, "Carlos, the lamp is in the basement. I'm cooking some pasta and sauce right now. I can't leave the kitchen. Let me tell you how to get to the basement and the room with the lamp."

She walked with me from her living room to the basement door and said, "Just go down the stairs to the basement. Turn the lights on and walk straight past four doors. At the end of the hallway, in the last room, you will see a tall gold lamp in the corner against the wall. You will see what happened. I need to go back to my cooking while you fix my lamp, okay?"

I said, "Yes ma'am, that's fine."

I went downstairs. When I arrived in the basement, I started walking to the last room as she described. I walked past four doors before I arrived and turned on the overhead light. I saw the lamp in one corner of the room. It was a tall lamp, gold-colored, Italian style, with a cream lampshade, and a little piece broken off.

I checked the lamp and knew I could fix it. I went upstairs and told her, "Ma'am, fixing this lamp will take me around forty-five minutes because it's a very detailed job. I'm going to have to go to my car and get my tools. I can start working on it right away. As soon as I finish, I will let you know, okay?"

The woman said, "Okay, just let me know when you finished, and I will come downstairs."

I retrieved my tools and worked on the lamp. Forty-five minutes later, the lamp was fixed. I went to get her. We both returned to the basement. She inspected the lamp and she liked it.

She said, "Oh my goodness! It looks wonderful. Well, I guess everything is fine, now. Thank you so very much."

We both smiled and walked out of the room. We walked down the hall and as we passed the first room, she turned off the light. When we passed the second room, she turned off the light. We passed the third room and again, she turned off the light. When we finally passed the last room, the fourth one, the stairs were just ahead of us. The customer walked in front of me ready to turn off the last light of the last room and right before she did that, I happened to look to my left and I saw a big painting on the wall. This painting was about seven feet high by five feet long. I couldn't believe it. The painting was my entire dream and everything that happened to me just a few nights before.

The painting was divided into two parts. The top part of the painting was a scene of a huge golf course garden. It had green grass, a flat terrain, blue skies, and an image of Jesus standing in the middle of the garden. Around him were hundreds of people dressed in white robes, just like in my dream. Jesus held a red umbrella in his hand that was open and positioned above his head. At the bottom of the painting was a beach, and Jesus was shown there again, standing in water up to his waist, and guess what! Behind him were several dolphins jumping in the background.

In that part of the painting, Jesus was waiting for everybody from the top of the picture in heaven to come down the hill to the beach at the bottom of the painting. They were going into the water one by one to be baptized by Jesus.

As soon I saw and contemplated this picture, I started crying and I thought, "Oh no. This is overwhelming."

I asked God, out loud, "Hey hold on, what are you trying to tell me?"

At that moment, the customer called to me from upstairs, "Hey Carlos. Are you okay?"

I said, "Yes. I'm fine," but she came downstairs anyway to check on me.

She looked at me and asked, "Are you okay? What's happening? What's going on with you?"

I was completely overwhelmed. Tears of joy rolled down my cheek. I looked at my customer and said, "This is impossible. This whole painting is almost exactly the same as the dream I had last Sunday. Excuse me, ma'am, where did you get this painting from?"

Confused, she said to me, "Well, three years ago a friend of mine came to the basement with this big canvas and started doing this painting. When he finished it, he said it was a gift for my family. The canvas was so big that I didn't have any other space in my house to put it. The only place this picture could fit was over here on that wall in the basement. Here, let me turn more lights on. Would you like to take some pictures of it?"

I said, "Yes sure. Thank you, ma'am."

I was really pleased with her generosity in letting me take a couple of pictures. I did and I thanked her again before leaving her home.

A few days later, I told my story to a friend of mine and he became fascinated with my testimony.

He said, "Carlos, please, you need to go to church and tell your testimony to everyone."

I said, "No, are you crazy? Nobody is going to believe me. I prefer to keep this story to myself and for all the people who were on the beach that day. No way."

My friend insisted several times, until I said, "Okay, but just one time, okay?"

He said, "Perfect."

That Sunday, I went to his house. He lived an hour away from me. It was a nice ride through the mountains. When I arrived at his house, he and his wife were waiting for me and together we started looking for a church nearby. I searched online for the closest church.

"Hey Google, take me to the closest Catholic church near here."

Google assistant responded, "The closest Catholic church in this area is St. Michael the Archangel."

We got in my car and I drove there. It was a late Sunday afternoon and when we arrived, the church looked closed. I drove around the church looking for a sign or some cars, but the only thing that we saw were the lights turned on inside the church. Oddly, there were no cars in the parking lot. Just then we saw a man. I don't even know where he came from, but he was running to the church and opened one of the doors.

I told my friend, "Let's follow him."

I parked my car and we ran to the same door this man opened and entered the church.

As soon as we stepped inside, we looked for the man ahead of us who ran into the building, but we couldn't find him. We didn't see anyone. To our surprise, we discovered the church was under some construction. There were no chairs or pews in the church. It was a big empty carpeted room with an altar at the end. An image of Jesus hung above the altar.

My friend said, "Let's at least pray since we are already here."

We were about to pray when the man appeared again. He looked like he was working at the church.

He said, "Hey guys, good evening. Can I help you with anything?"

My friend said, "Yes, we just need to pray. Is it okay even if it's under construction?"

He smiled and said, "Well guys, welcome to St. Michael Archangel Church. We have a chapel that has seats and it's not under construction. You guys can pray there."

We followed him as he opened a door to a beautiful little chapel. It looked brand new. The smell of fresh paint was very strong to my nose. There were chairs and an image of Jesus, perfect for prayer. We sat down and prayed for about ten minutes. When we finished our prayers and stepped outside the chapel, the church gentleman was there waiting for us.

He said, "Well, you guys are lucky because you came on the day before this church opens again. Let me explain to you guys. This church is connected to the new church through a hallway. The opening is tomorrow. Let me check if the hallway door is open so you guys can see how beautiful it is."

We followed him down the hallway and found the doors unlocked. He motioned for us to come in. As soon as the doors opened it revealed a huge statue of Saint Michael Archangel. It was amazing. I was in awe of Archangel Michael in all his splendor. My friend and I knelt and prayed for a few minutes.

When we finished praying, the man asked us, "Hey guys, what are you going to do now?"

I said, "Sir, it's getting late. So we will go home."

He said, "Wait a minute. I know it's getting late, but because tomorrow is the opening of the new church, the youth group is practicing for a play that will be presented tomorrow for the opening ceremony. Do you guys want to see it?"

Because this guy was so excited to show us what his group prepared, even though I was super tired, I didn't want him to feel bad, so I said, "Okay, that's fine. Take us there to meet your group."

There were twenty or so young people practicing for their performance the next day. My friend and I sat down and watched them. A few minutes passed and I felt my inner voice say, "Come on, Carlos. It's time to tell these guys your story, so they can get inspired, motivated, and strengthen their faith, so they can perform better tomorrow."

After I heard that in my mind, I waved to the man who took us over there and asked him, "Excuse me, do you think it is possible for me to give an inspiring testimony to your group before I leave?"

The man said, "Yes! Sure, anyways my group needs to take a break in a few minutes before we go over the play again, and at that point, you can tell them your testimony."

I agreed and after about five minutes, he called everyone over and they stood in a circle around me. He put a chair in the middle of the circle and told me when I was ready I could tell them my testimony. When everyone settled in, I began my story.

As I told them what happened, I could see in their faces how intrigued and in suspense they each were. I was in the middle of my story when a seventeen-year-old girl stood up and raised her hand.

She said, "Excuse me. Excuse me, sir. I'm sorry to interrupt your story, but I want to ask you a question? How was Jesus standing with you?"

I said, "He was behind me and I was in front of Him and He was holding me up, hugging me in a way, from behind. Why do you want to know that?"

She said, "Well, I have something that will blow your mind. It could be a coincidence, or it could be a sign, or a confirmation, about your story. I don't know, but you guys can judge for yourself."

I asked her, "What is it?"

She said, "Wait a minute; you will see. Let me show you."

She was a skinny girl, about 5'5" feet tall, with long hair. She rolled her head to the side and slowly turned around to show me a picture printed on the back of her T-shirt. She pulled her hair to one side and as she revealed the design I heard everybody gasp. Their mouths and eyes opened wide. When she revealed the back of the T-shirt it was an image of Jesus holding a man from behind.

Jesus, dressed in a white holy robe, had a bright light behind Him. The man He was holding was a white man, with brown hair, in his mid-twenties, with an expression on his face of surrendering in pain. The man was holding a hammer in one hand and a big nail in the other. He was dressed in blue jeans and a purple T-shirt. He was passing out, but Jesus was behind him grabbing and holding him, with compassion on His face. Below their feet was a tiny river of blood flowing from behind Jesus. On the side of the image were white beautiful flowers called lilies.

We all stared at the image. It was a stunning religious painting by Thomas Blackshear called *Forgiven*, but I didn't know that at the time. The painting depicts a man who has gone as far as he can go on his own and now seeks forgiveness, comfort, relief, grace, and mercy from the Messiah, Jesus Christ. (Blackshear and Lessin, 1996)

The young people looked at me as if to say, "Do you and this girl with the T-shirt know each other?"

I responded out loud, "No, this is the first time I've seen her. I guess this is a confirmation of the whole story for you guys so you believe what I'm saying."

From that day forward, a new phase of my life began. Every day, little miracles started showing up in my life. In the beginning I was afraid because all these events were hard to swallow. With time, I understood I always needed to remember the promise I made on the beach—I told God I would give my life to Him and from that moment He would be the captain of my soul.

The miracles continued, left and right, and proved to me everything that was happening was real. I needed to continue with the plan Jesus shared with me in heaven—to help people change their lives. He never told me how to do it, but I knew I would have to nurture that purpose the best way I could. My path had a new vision. With happiness in my heart, I would show people how important love was in our lives and how we could use love to heal.

CHAPTER 9

MOTHER TERESA OF CALCUTTA

—

Two months after my dolphin encounter, around the first week of July, everyone enjoyed the weather outside. Kids were having a blast enjoying the outdoors. I enjoyed the warm weather too, but on that summer day, I didn't know I would have another encounter. This time. it was with a holy encounter that would connect the experience I had in heaven with my own story. It seemed like it was a message from the divine to let me know everything that was happening to me had a sequence and a meaning. I wasn't prepared for what was coming my way.

It was Friday afternoon. I left my office around 2:00 p.m. and because the weekend was approaching, I decided to stop at the grocery store to buy some food for the weekend. I drove twenty minutes to the grocery store. I parked my car and started walking to the main entrance of the store. All of a sudden my phone rang. I reached for my phone and I answered the call. It was my sister Jennifer, who lives in Florida. She is a schoolteacher for an elementary school.

"Hey, Jenny. Good afternoon. How are you doing?"

Jenny replied, "Hey, I'm fine. I just have a break, so I'm calling to see how your day is going, and if are you planning something for the weekend."

"My day is going fine. Thank you and no, I don't have any plans for the weekend, just staying at home, cooking, resting, and watching movies. That's all, nothing special. What about you?" I asked.

"Well, you know, as a school teacher, I have a lot of work to be entertained all weekend—correcting all the exams I did for my kids last week, plus I have to make my agenda for the week and my school plans for next week—but if you want to be at home all weekend watching movies, I'm going to recommend a movie I know you will enjoy."

"Sure," I said. "What's the name of the movie? And, what is the movie about?"

"The movie is called *The Letters*. It's about Mother Teresa of Calcutta and how she wrote some letters to God to express her feelings. This is a real case and you won't believe what she wrote in those letters. I know you will enjoy the movie."

I said, "Okay, sounds good."

I remembered hearing stories about Mother Teresa when I studied in my Catholic elementary school. According to her biography, Mother Teresa (1910–1997), was a Roman Catholic nun who devoted her life to serving the poor and destitute around the world. She spent many years in Calcutta, India, and in 1950, she established the Missionaries of Charity, a religious congregation formed within the Catholic church. This organization provided aid for the most vulnerable and disadvantaged in society—those whom society often looks down upon.

Mother Teresa's selfless dedication to charity work has been recognized around the world. In 1971, she was awarded the Pope John XXIII Peace Prize, and in 1979, she received the Nobel Peace Prize. However, Mother Teresa chose not to attend the traditional ceremonial banquet and instead requested the funds be donated to the poor in India. Six years later, she was recognized by President Ronald Reagan when he awarded her with the Presidential Medal of Freedom.

I remembered what an incredible human being Mother Teresa was and I told my sister on the phone I would rent the movie as soon I got home. I became intrigued about what kind of letters she wrote to God.

At this point, we continued talking as I walked to the store. As soon as I neared the store's main entrance, the glass doors opened in front of me and I couldn't believe what I saw. My eyes opened wide. My jaw dropped and my phone slipped out of my hand. Guess who was coming out of the store?

I exclaimed, "Oh my God. Oh my God. This is not happening."

I picked up my phone and told my sister, "You won't believe who is coming out of the store right now, but I don't have time to tell you. I'll call you right back."

Then, I hung up the phone and watched as three nuns dressed like Mother Teresa of Calcutta walked out of the store. This all happened at the exact same time my sister was telling me about the Mother Teresa movie. I felt submerged in the twilight zone.

I stepped in front of the Catholic nuns and said, "Excuse me. Excuse me. Good afternoon. Nice to meet you. My name is Carlos; may I ask you a question, please?"

The three nuns said, at the same time, "Yes."

I continued, "Are you from the Mother Teresa congregation?"

One of them replied, "Yes."

"Are you from Calcutta, India?"

"Yes."

I asked if they were on vacation in Atlanta and one of them replied they lived in Atlanta.

So, I continued asking, "You live in Atlanta? Where?"

"In Little Five Points, Atlanta, at the Missionaries of Charity Gift of Grace House."

My mouth dropped again. I was speechless. I couldn't believe what was happening. I shook my face and told them I'd been living in Atlanta for more than twenty years and I never knew they were here. I asked them how long they'd existed.

One of the nuns said, "I'm Mother Maria. Let me tell you the story." She went on to say the *Georgia Bulletin* recently published an article describing how the Missionaries of Charity formally arrived in Atlanta in 1993 and began work in the archdiocese.

The Missionaries of Charity run the Gift of Grace House for women with AIDS, which opened in 1994 after volunteers helped renovate the two-story home. It is a safe place for women who were once homeless. Mother Teresa came to Atlanta in mid-June 1995 to mark the official opening of the house.

In addition to the work at the house, the white and blue sari-clad sisters help families at Colony South Trailer Park and are catechists at San Felipe de Jesus Mission, both in the Forest Park area. They also assist refugees in Clarkston, providing after-school programs, summer camps, and English classes.

After Sister Maria told me this story, I asked her if I could visit them. She said yes and said they were looking for volunteers to help with a summer camp. She said if I wanted to visit I should look for their address and phone number online. She suggested I call first to make sure they would be at the center before I went.

I told Sister Maria I had a Saturday off in two weeks. I said I would pass by then.

After this encounter, I was amazed! I must be dreaming. First, my sister called to recommend a movie about Mother Teresa, and then I walked into the store and met three of Mother Teresa's nuns who invited me to visit them at their center in Atlanta. It was unbelievable.

Two weeks later, I told another friend, Valentina, about my encounter with the nuns. After she heard my story, she asked if she could come with me. She was very intrigued to see this center we didn't know existed.

The weekend finally arrived and Valentina and I drove thirty minutes to the center. It was a beautiful yellow building, with white crown molding, two stories, lots of windows, and a beautiful garden in front of the house, full of flowers, roses, margaritas, and other kinds of yellow flowers. In the middle of the garden was a big white statue of the Virgin Mary with two white angels on either side.

Valentina and I walked to the front door and rang the bell twice. We waited for about three minutes, but no one came to the door. I thought no one was inside, so I walked around the house to see if they were outside. Then, I saw a young man on a ladder painting the side of the house. He saw me coming. He put his paint roller away and he asked me if I needed help. I told him I was looking for Sister Maria.

He said, "Oh yes. Sister Maria. Give me a minute and I will call her for you."

Valentina and I stood outside the house waiting for Sister Maria. After about five minutes, she appeared with two other sisters by her side.

Sister Maria said, "Hey Carlos. Thank you for coming. I'm glad you came to visit us. Who is your friend?"

"Thank you, Sister Maria. I promised you I would come today and here I am. This is my friend, Valentina. She really wanted to come with me to meet you and visit the center. She admired the life and miracles of Mother Teresa."

Sister Maria said, "Wow, that's great Valentina. Thank you for coming."

Valentina said, "It is a pleasure and an honor to be here, honoring the legacy of Mother Teresa."

Sister Maria said, "Let me give you a tour. Carlos, we are going to have to leave you here on the patio. You can sit down on a chair and wait for us. Your friend, Valentina, and I are going in the house. However, since this is a center for women only, we don't allow men inside the house. The purpose of this center is to take care of women with AIDS. I'm going to show Valentina how the other sisters work inside of the house and the kitchen. Then, we will come out and I'll give you both a tour outside of the house."

I said I would wait for them outside and they went in the house for around fifteen minutes. When they came out, Sister Maria gave us both a tour of their garden, their classrooms, and their little chapel.

When she finished, Sister Maria said to me, "Carlos, I want to introduce you to our Mother Superior. She is the principal of our community here. Come with me to her office. She is waiting for you there."

Sister Maria, Valentina, and I walked to the back of the house to the office of the Mother Superior. It was located just behind the women's center, in a second annex building where the sisters have their apartments and where the classrooms and administration office are located.

As soon I entered the Mother Superior's office, she received me with a very big smile and introduced herself. She said, "You must be Carlos, right?"

I said yes.

She continued, "The sisters told me about you, but tell me Carlos, a young man like you, what motivates you to visit a place like this?"

I said, "Mother Superior, I studied all my childhood in a Catholic school, and we used to read a lot about Mother Teresa of Calcutta and all the good she brought to humanity through her social work."

The Mother Superior said, "Oh that's nice to hear, but Carlos, tell me... have you ever felt a call to help the poor? Have you ever heard, deep in your heart, the call from Jesus?"

I said, "Of course, Mother, but to illustrate this to you I have a story to tell that will make you understand what I'm doing here."

Then, I told her my dolphin story and when I when to church to tell my testimony for the first time. I also told her about what happened at the church, about the girl who stood up, and asked me to describe my dream and give her some details about my encounter with Jesus—the same girl with long black hair who was wearing a T-shirt with the photo of Jesus called *Forgiven*, by Thomas Blackshear, on the back.

As soon as I said this to the Mother Superior, I reached in my pocket and took out a stamp with an image of Jesus. I showed it to her and she almost passed out.

She opened her eyes as wide as she could and said, "Oh my God, this is a miracle."

"What are you talking about, Mother? I asked.

She looked at me, with tears in her eyes, and said, "Carlos, now I know what you are doing here, my son. Now it is clear to me that Jesus sent you here to show us a confirmation of an event for which we are preparing."

Then, she started praying aloud and when she finished the first prayer she called all the nuns.

"Sisters, sisters!" she yelled. "Can everybody come to my office, please!"

At that moment. I was totally confused because I didn't know what she meant.

I said to her, "No, Mother. Jesus didn't send me here. I came because I met Sister Maria and two other sisters at the grocery store and they invited me here."

She waved her hand and said, "No, Carlos."

Then, again she yelled, "Sisters! Maria! Sister! Maria, please call all the sisters and bring everybody to my office, please."

One by one, the sisters started filing into the office until the last one arrived.

Then, Mother Superior said, "I called everyone to my office because I want you to see with your eyes the image that Carlos brought with him. He just shared a story where he dreamt he was with Jesus and how He showed up to him just like in this painting he is about to show you."

Then, she asked me to show everyone the stamp of Jesus I brought with me. I slowly pulled the image out of my pocket and showed it to all the sisters in the room. All the sisters were excited when they saw the picture.

Mother Superior said, "That's right. This is a clear message, a message that we have been waiting for. That's why we are going to pray now sisters."

They prayed a rosary for several minutes.

When they finished, Mother Superior looked me straight in the eyes and said, "Look, Carlos, even if I try to explain this to you one hundred times, you won't believe me or understand what I'm talking about, but I want you to discover by yourself what I just told you."

She handed me a pair of scissors and asked me to take them from her. Then, she asked me to open the big box on the floor behind me.

I carefully opened the box. I didn't know what was inside. I was nervous and excited at the same time. As soon as the box opened, I saw what was inside. Guess what it was?

I removed a T-shirt from the box and all the T-shirts were printed with the same image of Jesus from my dream and the girl's T-shirt at the church.

Then Mother Superior said, "Carlos, you don't know, but in two weeks we have a spiritual retreat here for young kids and teenagers. We prayed and asked God for a sign that the retreat would be a success. Then, you show up with that image. The same image we choose to be the theme or image at the spiritual retreat."

"Every day I'm more amazed at how God works in mysterious ways," she added.

After I left the Mother Teresa center, I was amazed, and I started to reflect on what happened. I thought this was not only a message for the nuns, but also for me too. I am to continue following this path. Day by day everything I am supposed to do will unfold before my eyes. It is another confirmation the Divine is with me and with you too, every time. I need to trust my spiritual journey. I need to believe, from the bottom of my heart, and start manifesting more scenarios like this, everywhere I go.

CHAPTER 10

FORTY DOLLARS

———

One of the most enjoyable seasons for me is fall. That's when the trees in Georgia change colors, from green to orange, yellow, and red; plus, the breeze of the cold weather arrives in the south.

One fall Sunday morning, a year after my experience with the dolphin, I received a call from the same family that went with me to Shell Island—the same family that lived through the odyssey of my rescue and the dolphin story. They invited me to join them for breakfast that morning at an Italian restaurant, not too far from my house. They wanted to meet around 9:00 a.m. and said they were missing me and wanted to spend time together.

I went to see them at the restaurant and we had a great time; the breakfast was delicious. While I was there, I received a message from another friend of mine, Austin, who was going to check my first book manuscript that night at 7:00 p.m. He told me to meet him at a restaurant that he would be at with his roommates, Chelsi and Noland.

Austin is one of my friends who enjoys reading books. He has a huge bookshelf full of a wide variety of books in his house and he is always reading something,

He also was a very methodical and analytical person. He wanted to give me a hand and help me make my book a reality. He was trying to act as an editor. After all, I didn't have good experiences in the past with some editors whom I found online. They were just scammers who took advantage of me, instead of helping me and giving me some advice on the production of my book. They just took my money and did a mess with my book manuscript. It made me extremely disappointed and discouraged about making my book a reality.

I knew Austin was different. He would help me. I knew this because he has a big heart and is the kind of person who doesn't have a filter and will tell you what he thinks. He always says being honest with another person helps them realize what they are doing so they can change for the better. Austin was in the military and served the country for several years in Iraq. He is a person of integrity and honor, a person who shows me true friendship by giving me good advice about life, and a person who I will trust with my book. I knew he would tell me what he genuinely thought about it—that he would be honest. That was what I really needed at that time.

Austin wanted me to give him the first part of the manuscript that afternoon, so he could start reading it and give me his point of view and review of my story. He wanted me to meet him at a famous Japanese sushi restaurant for dinner. I had never heard of the restaurant before.

After I finished my call with Austin, confirming I was going to see him and his roommates at 7:00 p.m., I continued eating my breakfast with my friends. Then, Jorge asked me if I had any plans that day. I told him I had a meditation for an hour at 12:00 p.m. with some friends, but after that, I would be free until 7:00 p.m. when I would meet Austin and his roommates for dinner. It was Sunday and I wanted to go hangout with my friends.

"Jorge, look, I have almost all day free to do anything after noon. What about you guys?" I asked Jorge and his family.

They said the same.

I started looking on my phone for things to do, something fun. I found that a Native American festival, the Pow Wow, was in town for that weekend only as they come just once a year. We decided to go to the festival. It was all day Sunday from 9:00 a.m. to 6:00 p.m. at Stone Mountain Park, so we had plenty of time to enjoy the festival. We decided to meet there at 1:30 p.m.

First, however, I went to my sound bath meditation. This was basically a meditative experience where those in attendance were "bathed" in sound waves. Various sources produced the waves, including healing instruments such as gongs, singing bowls, percussion, chimes, rattles, tuning forks, and even the human voice itself. (Gould, 2021) I had a wonderful and relaxing time.

After the meditation, I had a few minutes to spare so I looked up the restaurant where I was to meet Austin later. I found the restaurant online and realized it was right around the corner from the meditation place. I thought, *what a coincidence this place is just around the corner. That's great!*

I decided to drive by and check it out so I knew where I was going. I parked outside, walked to the main entrance, opened the restaurant door and the menu was there on a big sign, next to a woman sitting at a desk.

She said, "I'm sorry, sir, but we are closed to the public now. We will reopen for dinner time, from 5:00 to 10:00 p.m."

The woman was the restaurant hostess. She asked nicely if I had any questions. I wanted to know what kind of restaurant it was. I told her it was very pretty.

She said, "This is a very exclusive and unique sushi restaurant because we have several chefs located in different areas of the restaurant. You will try a special little menu from each chef at the different stations. That's why our prices are a little bit different from any other restaurant. The regular dinner plate is all inclusive for forty dollars. You will have the opportunity to taste every meal from every chef."

I said, "Oh wow. Thank you. That's awesome!"

At that moment, I thought this restaurant was too fancy for me. I said to myself *wait a minute. I don't even like sushi that much to pay forty dollars for something I don't even regularly eat. I think I will pass this time and I will tell Austin I will see him after dinner."*

As soon I arrived at the festival to meet my other friends, I parked my car and called Austin.

"Look, brother, I will meet you after dinner. I'm not in the mood for sushi today," I laughed. "I will see you at a coffee shop near the restaurant."

He said, "Carlos, are you sure? This is the best sushi restaurant I know in the city and you will enjoy this food a lot. Plus, we need to celebrate that you finally are going to give me your book manuscript for me to take a look and help you in this journey of making this book."

I said, "Yes, brother I'm sure. Let me be honest, I live on a very tight budget and I can't afford to pay for a fancy dinner like that. Someday, somehow, I will have the opportunity to eat in that restaurant again with you, but not today brother."

"Are you sure?"

"Yes, I'm sure," I said.

I hung up the phone and walked to the festival area where I bought my ticket. I called my friends to see where they were and as they arrived earlier, they were waiting for me at the arena area. They said they had a seat saved for me.

Jorge asked me, "How long will you stay with us at the festival, Carlos?"

"Well," I said, "I am invited to a dinner, but I didn't have the luxury to spend $40 on sushi with my salary."

Jorge suggested I stay with them until it was time for me to meet Austin and his friends for coffee.

I went with them and we had an amazing time listening to Native American music, dancing groups, storytelling. It was a wonderful event we all enjoyed.

At the end of the afternoon, when the festival came to an end, my friends asked me if I was hungry. It was 6:00 p.m., almost dinner time, and they were thinking about cooking dinner at home. They invited me to join them, but I politely declined.

Jorge said, "It's okay, Carlos. We are not going to charge you forty dollars. We will just charge you twenty dollars for our dinner." He started laughing and added, "That's a joke, brother."

I said, "Ah, you scared me for a second." Then, I laughed as well.

We started leaving the festival, walking toward the parking lot, when suddenly a very heavy wind started blowing in the area. It was fall, so dry leaves were flying everywhere. As I saw this happening, I started walking even faster to my car. While I was walking, the wind carried a paper toward me and it landed in front of my shoes.

My friends who were behind me asked, "What is that paper on your shoes, Carlos?"

"I don't know; let me take a look," I said.

I bent down and grabbed the paper. It was folded down into the size of a golf ball. I unraveled the page, which turned out to be a piece of notebook paper with something inside it.

I was in shock. I said, "Wait, what? No way! No way!"

My friends behind me start asking what was going on. They asked what was on the paper.

"You are not going to believe it guys," I said.

Inside the paper were two twenty-dollar bills crisscrossed. Not ten dollars. Not thirty dollars. Not fifty dollars. Exactly forty dollars—the precise amount of money I needed to go to the sushi restaurant, get dinner, and give my manuscript to my friend, Austin.

I turned around and with my mouth wide open, I showed the forty dollars to my friends. I said, "Oh, I guess God wants me to go to the sushi dinner."

My friends laughed and had such a kick out of the miracle. They started yelling, "No way! No way!" Then, they started jumping around. They were freaking out and laughing at the same time.

After this unusual incident, I hugged my friends, got in my car, called Austin, and told him what just happened to me. He also couldn't believe it.

He said, "Really? Well, come on. My roommates and I will wait for you to get dinner so we can eat together. Then, you will come home with us and I will make some coffee and start checking your manuscript. Now I'm even more intrigued about the magic that brought the money to you so you could come with us and I could check your paperwork."

Let me tell you, the dinner was amazing, It was the best sushi I have ever had. We had a great meeting and I felt very happy God found another way to make possible the impossible.

CHAPTER 11

AQUARIUM

___

On January 17, 2018, on a cold winter morning, I woke up around 5:00 a.m. and was still on my bed when suddenly I heard my inner voice telling me, *Carlos, today you need to go to the beach and enjoy the ocean. It's Saturday morning and you can make it to the beach early. It's time to go.*

I didn't listen. I thought I could sleep more and I started covering myself with the blankets. I wanted to continue sleeping, but my inner voice was very insistent. *Go to the beach*, it said. *Go to the beach. Go. Go. Go.* The message was so persistent that I got up, walked to my living room, sat down at my computer, turned it on, and started searching for a place to stay on the beach.

The closest beach for me to travel to is Panama City Beach, Florida, just five hours away from Atlanta, a beautiful waterfront town and vacation destination in Northwest Florida. A lot of people go there for its famous miles of white sand beaches, fronting the crystal waters of the Gulf of Mexico. When you get there, you feel like you are on an island in the Caribbean.

I started looking and searching, trying to choose between dozens of hotels and looking for a good deal. As I scrolled down the hotel pages, one flashed a special offer for that weekend. I clicked on it and opened the page. It was a nice hotel with a big room, a huge bed with a balcony in front of the beach, an infinity pool, and a continental breakfast. It looked perfect.

Before booking a hotel, I always check the online reviews as they never seem to fail. I like to travel out of the city on weekends in the spring and summer and, believe me, I rely a lot on the reviews because the majority of what they say is the truth. After I checked the reviews for this hotel, I was ready to go. I booked the room, got in my car, and drove five hours to Panama City Beach.

As soon as I arrived in Florida, I started playing some relaxing music. I rolled down my car window and let the warm breeze touch my face. It was a nice sensation. The five hour trip was coming to an end and my GPS navigation system started announcing I was nearing my destination.

Finally, I saw the name of the hotel off in the distance and I knew my weekend was about to start. I noticed the hotel was on the main road—front beach road—on the oceanfront. I saw a big parking lot where my GPS directed me. I parked my car, grabbed my wallet, cell phone, and bottle of water, and I was ready to get out of my car when suddenly something caught my attention out of the corner of my eye. I looked out my rear-view mirror and I couldn't believe what I saw. My mouth dropped open and I took a deep breath.

Guess what it was? Any idea? No? Well, it was a big-ass dolphin sign behind me. I couldn't believe it! Across the street from my hotel was an amazing aquarium for me to see and visit. Even if I planned it, it couldn't be better than this. I felt like I was entering the twilight zone one more time. I knew I was there because something was coming for me. I didn't know what it was, but at the same time, I was intrigued and excited.

So, guess what I did? Instead of walking to the hotel lobby and checking in, I walked across the street and went to the aquarium. It was late in the afternoon, around 4:00 p.m., and I thought they might be closed. I reached the main door, pulled the handle, and found it was open. So, I stepped in.

There was a big lobby area where I saw two lines from the main door directing people to the information desk and from there to the register to buy the tickets to enter the aquarium. As I walked down the hall to the information desk, I saw a nice woman seated at the table. She asked me if I had any questions.

I said, "Yes. I know it's late, but what time do you close the park?"

She said, "Well, we are closing now, but we will reopen tomorrow morning at 9:00 a.m."

I said, "Really?"

"Yes," she said. "I'm sorry. We are closing."

I thanked her and as I started to walk away, I felt very disappointed.

Suddenly, I heard her say, "Excuse me, sir. Excuse me. Could you come back, please? If you want, you can buy your ticket now for when the park reopens tomorrow morning. You will be one of the first visitors to get in and can enjoy the park by yourself. Plus, I have good news. We have a winter special I'm going to offer you and you should take advantage of this special offer today because it's for a limited time only. The special is fifty percent off the regular ticket price to swim and interact with the dolphins for about an hour. Would you be interested in that?"

"Wow! Really?" I said. I was so amazed. Of course, I wanted that ticket, and guess what? I bought the ticket.

She said, "Be sure to be here on time, so we can make an introduction to the team that will be with you at the dolphin tank. Plus, we need to explain the safety procedure before you enter the water and you will need to fill out some safety and legal paperwork. Remember, dolphins are wild animals we train here, but the wild runs through their veins. There will be other people going at the same time who will join you in this experience, so please arrive on time. Okay?"

I said, "Don't worry. I can't wait until tomorrow. Believe me, I will be here on time. I'm very excited to interact with dolphins."

"Okay, Carlos. My staff and I will be here early waiting for you. Have a great rest of the afternoon and I will see you tomorrow."

I left there with a happy face and a great feeling of satisfaction. I would finally interact with dolphins after my last time in the middle of the ocean. I was ready for this adventure.

I walked across the street back to my hotel. I went to the lobby area to start my check in and couldn't wait for the morning. I was so excited to see dolphins again. That night, I sleep like a kid waiting to open their gift on Christmas morning.

The next day, I was super excited. I took a good shower, got dressed, and went back to the aquarium right on time.

To my surprise, as soon I arrived, I checked my ticket with one of the park staffers and she took me from the lobby to a big waiting room. She said I would have to change my clothes and put on a swimming suit. They had a closet full of swimsuits of every size, so she asked me for my size and gave me one. I was ready for the action.

About five minutes later, she came back to the room and told me I would have to wait for a group of people who were running late. So, I sat down and waited... and waited....and waited. I was the only one in the room.

Finally, after fifteen minutes of waiting, a dolphin trainer came into the room and said, "Hello, are you, Carlos?"

I said, "Yes."

"Good morning," she said. "My name is Jessica and I will be your guide during your dolphin experience. I'm sorry that you have been waiting for a while here, but I have news for you. The group that was supposed to come at the same time as you canceled their appointment. So, you will be by yourself with the dolphins and the trainers. Will that be okay with you?"

"Absolutely!" I said.

I thought, *I know what is happening. This is another divine intervention for me to have a more private and amazing experience with the dolphins.*

I thanked God for this fantastic opportunity.

After I completed all the liability forms, the trainer took me to the tank where the dolphin was, right there in the middle of the amphitheater. There was a professional photographer included with my ticket too.

"Wait. What?" I thought. "That's awesome!"

The trainers brought the dolphin next to me and the one-hour session started. The trainers taught me all about the dolphin's lifestyle and preferences. I wasn't nervous. I fed him. We played together. He gave me a kiss. I petted him. He even let me hold his dorsal fin while he swam around the pool.

I felt a strong connection with the dolphin. He brought me memories of when I was drowning in the middle of the ocean, and the way his dolphin brother saved me. Without any doubt, I knew from now on, dolphins were part of my life now. I felt grateful and honored to be with one of the species that saved me. This definitely was one of the most fun and grateful days of my life.

In the last ten minutes of our time together, I heard my inner voice say, *when you finish your book, the press release and book launch event will be here in this aquarium amphitheater with the dolphins. So go and tell the management.*

I couldn't believe it and I thought, "No way."

My inner voice knows how I resist this kind of message out of the blue, so it just gets persistent and louder. I heard the voice again say, *yep, you will be here.*

After so many experiences with these messages, even though I feel so strange sometimes and I don't want to do the things it says most of the time, it's usually right most of the time. We all have that little voice inside of us. Some people call it intuition, which tells us what to do and what not to do. Most of the time, we don't listen to this little voice, and, in the end, what happens is what the voice said would happen. I always end up saying, "Oh my God! If only I would heed the advice my inner voice gave me, the outcome to anything in my life would be different, right?" The voice always says what you should or shouldn't do. We need to listen carefully and follow our intuition. We just need to follow our hearts.

This time, I listened to my intuition. When my dolphin session ended, I thanked the photographer and the dolphin and got out of the pool.

As I exited the tank, I thanked the trainer and asked, "Excuse me Jessica, can I speak with your manager, please, for a minute? I just need to ask a question."

She looked at me with worry, and said, "Is there something wrong? Is everything okay?"

I reassured her, "Yes, I had a great time. I just need to speak with your manager. Everything was great with the dolphin encounter, thank you."

Jessica said, "Okay, take a good shower to wash off all the pool water while I go look for the manager and I will meet you in the lobby."

I said, "Okay. That sounds good to me. Thank you, Jessica."

I took a shower, got dressed, and went to the lobby. Jessica was there waiting for me.

"Carlos, there you are. The manager will see you in her office. Please follow me and I will take you there."

She then walked me to the manager's office where she invited me to sit down.

Jessica said, "Carlos, the manager will be here soon."

As I sat down, I started looking around. It was a big office. The interior was painted in light blue with photos of the ocean, dolphins, and whales. One wall was full of awards and family pictures.

Two minutes later, the manager walked in and said good morning. I introduced myself and asked her name.

"Martha," she said, "the operations manager of the aquarium."

She was a very nice woman in her fifties. She was around 5'7" tall and blonde, with a big smile on her face. She looked like a really nice person.

Martha said, "Did you have a good time, Carlos? How can I help you?"

I shifted in my seat and hoped I didn't sound too weird. I said, "I have a question to ask you, but before I do, I have to tell you my story. Do you have ten minutes or are you busy right now?"

She looked very curious and sat back in her chair as she said, "Yes, of course. Go ahead. I'm all ears."

I told her the whole story and she hung on to each word. In the end, she said, "Wow, Carlos. That was quite an amazing story." She paused, then remembered I had a question for her. "So, how can I help you? You still have a question for me, is that right?" she added.

I said, "Yes ma'am, that is right."

I took a deep breath and said, "You are not going to believe me, but when I was in the pool tank with your dolphin I got a message from my inner voice, which said as soon as my book is done the launch of my book will be here. I know—I couldn't believe it, but that's what I heard. Believe me, I was afraid to ask you, but something inside of me insisted I do and I thought to myself, 'What do I have to lose? Nothing, right?' That's when I made the decision to look for you and ask you this question. I have been writing a book about my story with the dolphin and this really would be a great place to present it. What do you think? Do you think it's possible?"

She smiled at me and said, "After hearing your story, we definitely would love to have you present your book here, Carlos. Let me know when your book is done and ready to launch and we will make a plan to make a presentation here at the aquarium. I will be glad to help you, Carlos."

As soon as she said that, tears of happiness rolled down my cheeks. I was just amazed how God continues to work in mysterious ways and how just being obedient to my inner voice took me to this point, where I proved one more time following my heart and intuition is the best way to end up with a great outcome.

I never expected anything like swimming with dolphins or asking to launch my book here. I was a complete stranger to this. How can this be happening to me? I felt so thankful. I had a lump in my throat. It was so easy for her to say yes right there on the spot. I guessed God had a plan.

As Martha walked me out of her office, she put her hand on my shoulder and said, "Carlos, we are all believers here. I understand what is happening and I want to support you and your messages. By the way, this aquarium has a chain in the Caribbean, and we will be glad to put your book here and in the other aquariums too."

I was shocked and smiled so wide. "Thank you, oh my God. Thank you so much!"

I left that place with inner peace in my heart, and a feeling that in this life, God has a plan and a purpose for everyone, and that plan will unfold to every one of us as long we feel the power in our heart and follow our inner voice and intuition. Life is a manifestation of miracles, every day and every moment. If we pay attention and look around we will be able to witness miracles everywhere around us.

CHAPTER 12

BEACH HOTEL

———

On Memorial Day weekend in 2018, I wanted to go back to the beach hotel where I stayed after my near-death experience. It was the three-year anniversary that weekend, so I travelled from Atlanta to Florida on Saturday morning. I checked in to the same hotel that afternoon.

The clerk at the desk, in a very polite way, saluted me and welcomed me to the hotel, She asked if I had a reservation. I did, so she asked me if I was ready to check in. I gave her my ID and my credit card and she started looking for my reservation online.

She looked up and asked, "Excuse me, sir. Have you ever stayed with us before?"

"Yes, I stayed here three years ago. I haven't been back since. I had an accident the last time I stayed here," I explained.

She looked at me with big eyes and said, "An accident? What happened? Can you tell me?"

I said, "Okay. I know there are people behind me, so I will be quick with the story."

I told her the edited version of my story and when I was at the part where I dropped to my knees and began praying, she started convulsing and having a real medical seizure, so much so, the other staff members came over and held her arms and body to hold her up so she wouldn't fall. She started sobbing.

I was scared. I didn't know what was happening and what I should do. I felt bad that my story was having that effect on her.

The staff calmed her down and I just stood there shocked. She composed herself, the other staff went back to work, and I was still standing at the counter.

She said, "You don't know what you just gave to me. You have given me hope. You have reconfirmed that God is here with me. You don't know who I am. I am not just a clerk here. I am the general manager of the hotel. I am here in this position because God wants me here. I am only a high school graduate. I have always been a good servant and good to people. I was promoted to leadership, bypassing other people with higher qualifications than me. My bosses said that my morals and ethics are what got me in these top positions. I always prayed to God to be with me and I would do the best that I can. He took me to professional positions that I never dreamed I could have. That's why I am here as the general manager. Now for you to be so nice to tell me your story and confirm my life to me, I am going to do something for you. I am going to give you the best suite of the hotel for you stay this weekend. I want you to have an amazing stay with us. Every time you come back here to the beach, I want you to stay with us and we will take good care of you."

This taught me I can never know the impact I have on another person and it's more important to help others than to keep it to myself. I felt that to tell the story wasn't enough. I wanted people to take it personally and to have a physical reminder of the messages of the story. So, I looked online for the image from my dream—the painting by Thomas Blackshear—the same image the teenager had on the back of her shirt. I found that image on a little prayer card the size of a business card. On one side, Jesus holds up a man and on the other side is a forgiveness prayer.

I feel forgiveness is very important. I know so many people have childhood trauma. A great way to get over that is through forgiveness. It's not for the other people; it's for ourselves to clean our hearts. To spread the message of hope, I also want to share a tool to freedom so we can all live a better life and be more kind to one another. I know forgiveness is a great tool to use for our self-healing. One thing I am doing to help others is handing out this prayer card every time I tell my story. I feel I'm planting a seed in that person's heart and from that moment, it is up to them to keep that seed alive, to take care of it, until it grows and transforms into a wonderful tree—big, strong, and beautiful.

During that hotel stay, I gave a card to every housekeeping woman I met. When I returned at the end of summer on a different trip, one of them came up to me in the hallway and said, "Are you the man who gave me that little card, the forgiveness card?"

I said, "Yes, I am that man. Why?"

She said, "Well when you handed me the card, you didn't really say anything. We didn't talk and you don't understand. The card meant so much to me. I was going through a lot of hard times then. I want to say thank you because you gave me hope when I needed it the most. You were the messenger; you brought me the message that I was wanting, that everything was going to be okay."

I could see she was in a good place and feeling good about her life and herself. I felt touched by what she said to me. I am glad to be of service to help people find their inner light so they can shine again.

CHAPTER 13

MYSTERIOUS BLUE BRACELET

———

Two weeks before the weekend of Labor Day 2018, Steven, an old friend whom I met on a spiritual retreat in Atlanta years ago, called me from Michigan to let me know he would be in town for the holiday. He would like to meet me for a coffee or lunch and he would be seeing other friends too.

He had been planning a trip to the South for a long time and finally, he had some time off from work. I asked him where he was staying and he said at a hotel in downtown Atlanta. I told him he was welcome to stay at my house if it was not too late to cancel his hotel reservation. He told me he would check on the reservation and call me back.

A short time later, he called me back. He could cancel his reservation and he accepted the offer to stay at my house. That way, he would save some money for himself and he was happy about that. Two weeks later, he flew to Atlanta and I went to the airport to pick him up.

On our way to my house, we stopped by an Italian restaurant and got some delicious four-cheese pasta. While at the restaurant, we started talking about how it had been three years since we last saw each other. We laughed about old times and naturally the conversation caught us up to the present.

After that, we went home and planned a tour of the city for the next day. The weekend was approaching and I told Steven, "The summer is about to end and the best thing I love to do every year is to enjoy these last days of summer at the beach. Let's plan a trip to Florida for the weekend. It's not too far from Atlanta, and believe me, we are going to have a good time."

That Friday, we woke up early in the morning and drove to Florida. Five hours later, around noon, we arrived in Panama City, a waterfront town and my favorite vacation destination in Northwest Florida. The city was full of tourists enjoying the last days of the hot summer. Our hotel was right on the beach. We checked in and we ran to the beach. The sand was as white as snow and hot because the day was clear with sunny skies. On the beach, the sand was so thin it looked like baby powder.

Steven and I jumped into the water and started swimming right away. The water was crystal clear and warm. We started enjoying the weather, the water, and the sun, for the rest of the day. We had a good time from the moment we got there. It was off the beaten path where we could relax a bit.

On the last day of our mini Florida vacation, we drove through the more active part of town to the most famous restaurant on the beach. This restaurant was like a resort, with a swimming pool in the middle and a stage on the side where they were presenting live music and DJs.

We arrived around 1:00 p.m. and we got some chairs at the restaurant right on the beach. From there you could see an amazing view, emerald crystal waters, sports activities, and beautiful people walking everywhere enjoying the great weather of the weekend.

After Steven and I ate some pizza, I went to my car to grab two extension chairs and a canopy. We thought we would spend the rest of the day on the beach. I opened my canopy and jumped into the ocean. I enjoyed the water for about an hour and a half when my friend called out to me.

"Carlos, come on. Come here. Do you want anything to drink? I'm buying."

"Really," I said. "Just a soda for me, thank you."

Steven said, "Hey Carlos, you won't believe me, but after almost two hours I'm hungry again. It must be the dehydration from the ocean. Let's get another little pizza."

"That's fine with me, brother. If you are hungry get your pizza," I said.

Steven said, "Let's go back to the restaurant bar on the beach and we can order it, please."

While we waited for our pizza, a young man around twenty-five years old showed up. He appeared intoxicated by the way his eyes were out of orbit. He ordered some pizza too and then he said hello to Steven and me. You could tell he was a good kid. You could feel his good energy, plus he sounded educated and he had good manners.

He said to us, "Hey guys. Nice to meet you. My name is Tyler and I came here with my wife and kids. Are you enjoying your time on the beach?"

Steven and I both said, yes.

Tyler continued, "I'm sorry guys. You are going to think I'm talking too much, but I'm just happy to have my family with me here at the beach. We are having a vacation of a lifetime in this beautiful place."

I said, "Good for you, Tyler."

"Plus," he said, "I'm celebrating my graduation from engineering school and I'm taking a break. I came with my family to enjoy the last holiday of the summer, Labor Day. So far, it has been great. We have a beach family house here too. My family and I always spend time here whenever we have a chance. Let me tell you guys, I know this town like the back of my hand. I have been coming here since I was a kid. If you need any directions or need any help looking for something to do and to have some fun, like karaoke, good restaurants, nightclubs, and festivals, ask me, because I know a lot of places to make your stay amazing."

Tyler's wife then called to him from a distance. She said, "Hey, let's go. We need to go back home. We need to go to a dinner later. Come on. Let's go, Tyler."

Tyler said, "Hey guys. Take my phone number. Let me know if there is anything you need."

At that moment, I was thinking, *this guy is too nice. Why is he insisting on being our friend? Maybe he is a drug dealer and he is trying to sell his drugs to us, but he has the wrong guys for that.*

I said, "Tyler, hurry up before your wife comes and takes you by the ear, like a kid." I started laughing.

"You are right, Carlos. You seem to know how my wife behaves," he said and he laughed too. "Hey, take a picture of me and attached it to my number. That way you know who it is and don't forget me guys," he added. Then, he laughed again.

I took the picture, so he could go with his wife and kids. When I checked it, I said, "Oh, wow. You look just like my trainer. What is your name again? So, I can put it here."

He responded, "C'mon, bro. Tyler."

I laughed and said, "Wait. What? You will not believe this, but guess what my trainer's name is? It's Tyler, too."

He smiled and said, "No way! Really?"

At that moment, we heard his wife yelling, "Tyler! Tyler! Tyler! We need to go!"

He said, "I got to go, guys. My captain is calling me. It was a pleasure to meet you guys." He started walking away and then turned around and said, "Hey, wait a minute. I want to give you guys something for good luck."

I looked at Steven with an expression that said, "Now what?" I said to him, "I don't know, bro."

Tyler said, "Okay. Extend your arm so I can put this lucky bracelet on you."

I extended my arm and he pulled a bracelet from his wrist. He put it on me and latched the blue bracelet on my wrist. He did the same with my friend.

Then he said, "That will bring you good luck in your life my friends. It was nice to meet you guys. God bless you," and he started walking away.

I couldn't even speak because I didn't understand why this young man, who came to us out of the blue, whom we didn't know, talked to my friend and me for ten minutes, and then gave us the gift of these bracelets. I was speechless. He walked away, smiling and waving his hand. He said, "Goodbye. God bless you guys and good luck in your lives."

I thought, *what the heck was that* and started laughing.

The waiter came with our pizza. Steven and I sat down and enjoyed it. After that incident, I walked to the beach and relaxed on the sand for an hour before we went back to Atlanta.

All the way from Florida to Georgia, I was thinking and wondering about the meaning of the bracelet. *Why did this man, who didn't even know me, give me this blue bracelet?* I was overthinking.

I asked myself, *why? Why? Maybe there is a spell on this bracelet... Oh my god!*

Maybe it is black magic! Oh Lord...

Or, maybe this bracelet has a message for me.

I started checking out the bracelet looking for a message, but there was none. The bracelet had a very tiny silver medal, the size of a tiny button. The medal had a letter on one side and on the other side it said, "PV enjoy life." When I arrived back home, I immediately went to my computer and started searching the following: "Blue bracelet, with a letter on one side, PV on the other side." I pressed the enter button and I waited a few seconds for the answer to appear.

My connection was slow that day and I waited longer than usual.

Different answers appeared, but nothing was close to the bracelet I wore. Then I had the idea to search the same question in images. I typed "blue bracelet with a silver medal and the initials PV" again in images on the Internet search bar, and many blue bracelets later I found a picture that matched my bracelet. I pressed the cursor on the picture and as soon as the picture opened with the exact blue bracelet I had on my wrist, a message appeared under the bracelet. Guess what this message said?

When I started reading the purpose behind that bracelet, I almost had a heart attack. I put my left hand on my chest, took a deep breath, and with my eyes wide open, I read the description in disbelief.

This was a random gift this mystery man, named Tyler, gave me on the beach. A young man whom I didn't know anything about and who didn't know anything about my life gave me this bracelet as a symbol of good luck. What I discovered next put tears of happiness in my eyes, because someway, somehow, I received a message from heaven, believe it or not.

The message on the computer screen under the bracelet said: "This bracelet is used to contribute to Save the Dolphins." The money raised through the sale of this bracelet (PV) will be donated to the Oceanic Preservation Society. which is dedicated to protecting our oceans and planet, including advocating for the protection of dolphins.

My eyes were watering; tears slid down my face. I couldn't believe what I was seeing. It was another synchronicity about my dolphin story—maybe a message from God or heaven telling me my purpose in life was so clear. Maybe I didn't want to hear it and they had to send a random person to deliver that message of hope to me—a message that one of my purposes in life will be helping these beautiful angels of the ocean. The dolphin message opened my heart to have faith again and to know anything is possible for those who believe.

CHAPTER 14

RETREAT

———

In July 2018, I went to the grocery store, as usual, to get my groceries for the following week. I was getting some vegetables in the produce section when all of a sudden I heard somebody yelling my name.

"Carlos! Carlos!"

I looked up, searching around looking for the person calling my name. Finally, I saw behind me, running at a distance, a friend of mine, Oscar. It had been almost a year since I'd last seen him. He finally caught up to where I was and we started talking.

'What's up, my friend? Long time no see. Hey, I'm in a hurry, but what are you doing this weekend?" he asked.

"Nothing special, Oscar."

"Well, I want to invite you to my birthday party this coming weekend. Do you think you can come?"

I said, "Yeah sure. That's fine, bro. I will be there."

Then, I remembered. The last time I heard from Oscar, he moved to a new house and I needed to ask him for the address.

"Hey, just give me your new address and I will be there, okay?" I said.

"Okay sure," he said. "I will send you a message to your phone. Do you still have the same phone number or did you change your phone number?"

I said, "I still have the same old number. You can send me the address there. Thank you, brother."

"Okay. I will see you there. Have a nice day and take care."

"Okay. Take care."

The days passed and Saturday arrived. I woke up that morning, took a shower, got a cup of coffee, went for a walk, then ate my breakfast, and when I looked at the clock, the morning had quickly gone by. It was almost noon. I called Oscar to check what time he wanted me to stop by. He said anytime. I didn't have anything else to do that day until I went to the party, so I decided just to go earlier. I grabbed my car, stopped at a bakery shop, and bought him a chocolate birthday cake.

Then I showed up at his house. As soon I got there, I walked to the front door and rang the bell. I was holding the chocolate cake in my hands when his mom opened the door.

She looked at me with surprise and exclaimed, "Carlos, my darling. What a surprise! I didn't know you were coming today."

She looked at me like I was a baby. She was happy and she gave me a big hug.

I went inside and walked to the kitchen with the cake in my hands and put it on the counter. In the kitchen, Oscar's mom, wife, sister, and his two kids, Jose Samuel and Kamila, sat at the table helping his mom with the decorations for the party. We started talking about how the year was going for everyone and how everything was fine. Then, little by little, Oscar's friends start coming to the party but I didn't know anybody else except Oscar's family, because he invited most of his coworkers and friends from home.

After two hours at the party, Oscar asked me if I could tell everyone the story of my near-death experience.

I thought, "Oh, boy. This isn't a testimony thing. It's a party. What if they don't want to hear this?"

"I don't think this is the right setting," I said to Oscar. "Brother, maybe I could do this another time. Everyone is dancing and having a good time. Why do you want me to do this here?"

Oscar replied, "No. No. I really want you to tell your story, please. I really love that story and you are a good storyteller. I know everyone will enjoy your story and the message at the end. Plus, that will be the best present you can give me for my birthday."

I said, "Okay, okay, gather everyone. Let's bring some chairs and get everyone to sit in a circle in the middle of the living room."

Oscar grabbed a wine glass and with a little spoon started tapping on it, making noises like a bell ringing and asking everyone for attention because he wanted me to tell my story.

Little by little, everyone on the outside patio started coming inside the house. The living room was the place with the most space so we gathered there, but it was getting full. Finally, when everyone was sitting in a circle, silence invaded the room.

At that moment, I stepped inside the circle and I presented myself. Then, I started telling my dolphin story.

To my surprise, everyone was eager to hear my testimony.

I started talking and telling everyone the story like I was on a camping trip with friends in the middle of the forest around a big bonfire, and for the next half hour, everyone at the party gave me their attention. At the end of my testimony, I felt some sorrow and heard someone crying. I started looking around the room wondering where all this sorrow was coming from.

To my surprise, I saw a family at the end of a hallway. There was a mother, a father, and two sons. The father waved me over and I wondered what was going on. When he saw me walking his way, the father started wiping tears from his face. I walked toward him and said, "Is everything okay? I'm sorry if my story made you cry. It wasn't my intention to make you feel like that, but everything is fine, you know. At least it had a happy ending."

The father's face changed to a happier one and he smiled at me.

"Yes! You are right," he said, as tears of compassion and happiness continued to fall on his cheeks.

Then he said, "Hey Carlos, that was a beautiful story. Thank you for sharing it. Now, I know why Oscar was eager for you to tell everyone your story at his party. It was very emotional and it touched every fiber of my heart. It really resonated with me. By the way, I am so excited that I forgot to introduce myself." We shook hands and he said, "Nice to meet you. My name is Sebastian and this is my family. Here is my wife and kids. It has been a pleasure to meet you and to hear your testimony."

"Let me tell you something, Carlos." he continued. "Did you know that you can touch a lot of people's hearts if you share your story in bigger places, and guess what? You don't know this, but I am one of the organizers of a big spiritual retreat that will take place two weeks from now. I really want you to come. I will pay for your ticket if you come and share your testimony."

In the beginning, I didn't want to go to the spiritual retreat because I didn't know what it was about and I had a lot of work that month. However, when he insisted and explained all the details to me, I agreed and he gave me all the information.

Two weeks later, that Friday was the day we would leave for the retreat. I met Sebastian at a church near my house. There was a school bus where fifty men climbed in and at 4:00 p.m. we headed out for our weekend adventure.

The coordinators tried to get us to sing songs and get to know each other. We were such a mixed group, from teenagers to elders, from landscape guys to executives and lawyers, family men and bachelors. All social classes, every color, every race, were all here. We didn't know each other and we weren't sure about the organizers, so we really didn't feel like singing.

The one common denominator was that we all wanted to see if there was a chance to bring back our faith in ourselves, in life, and maybe even in God. That was the promise of the retreat experience—to feel the divine in your heart and come out of the retreat totally rejuvenated to start a new life.

On the way to the retreat center, we left the city and the bus went deep into the mountains to a place apart from all civilization—a natural place surrounded by green mountains and beautiful tall trees all around. I couldn't really tell where we were. I felt so awkward because I was in a place to which I was invited, but I didn't know what it was all about. I didn't know what I was getting into, going on a school bus for hours with fifty strangers to spend three days with people who I didn't know. I kept asking myself, "What the heck am I doing here?" I was looking out the window wondering if the other cars would rescue me or if I should start waving my hands. Maybe I could make a sign that said, "Help!" I could hold it up to the window or maybe if the driver came to a stop, I could jump out the window. My best plan was to call an Uber or Lyft, the famous taxi services. I knew they would go anywhere to pick me up and rescue me. Ninety minutes later, up in the mountains, we arrived at the retreat center. It was in the middle of nowhere and when I checked my phone, it had no signal.

Trapped, I felt like there was no way to escape. So, I followed the group. When we got inside of a building, they collected all our cell phones and watches and put them in Ziplock bags. They said they would give them back to us at the end of the retreat.

Oh boy, what am I doing here? I thought.

During our first retreat meeting, they told us all the rules of the three-day event. They said a lot of miracles would be happening and they opened the little alter that holds the Blessed Sacrament, a devotional name used by Catholics that contains the bread called the body of Jesus. It's usually closed, but they explained it would stay open during the retreat and that was why we would receive extra blessings.

After that, they showed us to our rooms and gave us thirty minutes before we were to meet in the dining room for dinner. Then, the official beginning of the retreat would start.

I can't really share the whole weekend, but what I can tell you is that each of us experienced personal growth. They had classes in every area of life.

On the second day, one of the exercises was to hold the Bible with one hand underneath and the other one top. We were to ask out loud, in front of all the other men, one question we wanted to ask God.

So, I asked, "Okay, God, what I want to know is, will my book impact people's lives? Will people believe me?"

That was on Saturday. The supervisor said, "You will all have your answers tomorrow."

On Sunday, at the very last activity, they took us to a room with fifty scattered chairs.

They said, "Go ahead and sit in any chair."

On each chair was a letter-sized manila envelope. We each sat down and were instructed to put the envelope on our laps.

The director said, "Now, so you don't think that we planned anything, take your envelope and pass it to someone near you. It doesn't matter who, just hand it off to another person."

We followed his instructions. Then, he asked us to open the envelope we were holding.

He said, "These are the answers to the questions that you asked God about yesterday."

When I opened my envelope, I was stunned. My paper contained a cartoon drawn by kids at elementary school. There was a globe of planet earth and on the top there were people running around holding an open book. Pictured on the inside of the book were drawings of the Holy Spirit and Jesus, who looked like they were coming out of the book. All around them people from every country of the world were running around leaving streams of red hearts spreading all around the globe. It looked like love was spilling out of the book.

When I saw that picture my eyes started watering. I felt love and a sense of purpose. I knew I had to go on with this book. I could tell it was not just for me, but it was an important message for everyone to hear, beyond any borders. It's a message to us all for love, hope, and happiness.

Each of the fifty men at the retreat also received answers to their questions. We were so humbled to witness these miracles together. Every envelope contained a message that touched everyone's hearts in such a way we didn't need any more proof the divine was real. That was the purpose of the whole retreat.

Can you believe that at the end of the retreat we cried with happiness and no one wanted to leave? It was the most amazing experience of unity, love, and true community.

It was hard to believe at the beginning I was ready to bolt; I heard the other men were feeling the same. Here at the end, we felt so connected and went through this amazing experience together. It was life changing and we were so grateful.

At that moment, I had my question answered. That was all I needed to know. I was ready to start writing my book and tell my story to the world, even if at that time I didn't know how I would do it. From that day, I prayed and meditated for this book to become a reality.

PART 3

LIFE LESSONS

CHAPTER 15

KEEPING THE FAITH

I want to share with you the way prayer works in my life. I believe we should not only pray when we have a problem or when we need a miracle in our lives. Instead of waiting until the last minute to look for help through prayer, I believe we should pray all the time. We do not know what life will bring us every day. Each day is a mystery; it can bring a challenge.

Have faith. Each day is really an adventure because we do not know what will happen. In my case, since I was a child, my mom taught me how to pray. I also learned at my Catholic school. Eventually, I came to understand Jesus was my friend. I carried a card with the picture of Jesus in my pocket.

He became my best friend. Whenever someone picked on me or treated me poorly, I would walk away and look at the picture and have an inner talk with Jesus. As I got older, I left the card behind, because I knew Jesus was in my heart and I did not need the picture as a tool anymore.

I would ask in my heart, "Jesus, I need to talk with you please."

When I pray, I do not feel alone. I feel surrounded by love. I feel safe and secure. When I pray, I feel answers come to me. I feel heard—that help is on the way in divine timing.

Maybe it is not the answer which I was looking for, but somehow it works out in my favor even though I do not know how or why. One of the most powerful prayers I said was when I was fourteen and diagnosed with leukemia. I asked God to help me and I said it so loudly, as if I was talking to my best friend. In my heart, I felt God was listening to me.

I asked God, "Take this cancer away from me." I could feel a response right away; in every hair on my skin, I felt a wave of warmth and a sense of peace followed that invaded every cell of my being. I knew at that moment, the way I declared for God to heal me, the miracle would start to work on me.

What I am trying to say is we must feel it in our heart when we pray. We must mean it, that what we ask for will be given to us. We must believe we will receive blessings and protection.

The Bible says, "Ask, and it shall be given you," (KJV Matthew 7:7) and I recommend we "pray without ceasing." (KJV 1 Thessalonians 5:17). That is when we can have a sense of security and inner peace. The peace eventually fills our emotional hearts and our bodies too. I have seen amazing miracles happen with prayers, situations that suddenly changed beyond all odds. A prayer is a tool for life, always remember that.

In 2017, several friends introduced me to this amazing woman and teacher. Her name was Joyce Rennolds. She was a valued international speaker and author and was known as a "motivator of one or a thousand." She always brought inspiring motivational messages to every class and to her students and audiences.

She taught me one tool that changed my perception of life, scripting. This was a new concept for me, but it's quite simple. It's like a journal of your future. The first step is to find a notebook. Open the first page and dedicate the page to yourself. For example, I wrote something like this: I dedicate this scripting book to myself, to reach every goal in life, to live a wonderful life, to bring hope and new happiness to my life, and to find every reason to wake up every morning because I know the future will bring me what I want if I ask for it.

Scripting is as simple as just handwriting our needs or desires to God. You write your goals and aspirations in the present tense because it is important you describe what you want for your life, as if it is already happening. It's like writing a direct message to God. By writing it down, it becomes clearer.

I have had great success with this technique. I wrote about someone who treated me poorly. I wrote, "Dear God, I am asking for help. From today, now, I want (name) to treat me with respect and kindness. I know that this person is capable of this. I am having a good time with this person. We are laughing together. We respect each other and we are getting along very well. Thank you, God."

Start with something small, such as trying to find a parking spot at the grocery store and see how it works for you. You could write something like, "When I arrive tomorrow at the supermarket, I will find an empty space close to the entrance."

If you need a car or a partner, you can use this technique. If you want a car, describe what you want—what brand, color, size, make, and model you want, everything in detail. After you write it down, read it out loud. Speak it into existence. Imagine you are already driving this car. Use the power of your imagination to create this, We have this creative power that we don't even tap into.

We should script every day. People plan what they will do for vacation, but we really don't sit down and write about what we genuinely want to create with our lives. What is meaningful in your life? What would make you genuinely happy?

The best use of this technique is to create our lives so we are better people. We can ask for more patience, more understanding, better communication, and to stop procrastination. These are the things that will make our lives more enjoyable. It's not the car or the partner, it's inner peace and service to mankind that will give us the greatest satisfaction.

CHAPTER 16

CHOOSING HOPE

———

Many people go through hardships we don't know about. We don't know what's going on in their lives. Sometimes they smile and hide their feelings. They must work, play their roles, and tend to their responsibilities. You never know what someone else is going through in their life.

I've been there myself when I was a teenager. A lot of my friends at high school felt the same way—as if nobody understood us because most of our families didn't have time to pay attention to our problems and emotions at that age. We felt everything very intensely because we didn't have past experiences to compare our situations to and every problem seemed the end of the world.

I always reach the conclusion that my problems will pass. They are temporary. Everything in life is temporary. Nothing is eternal. Life is beautiful. I have a future to think about and that is it for me. That brings me around and I decide that I don't have to throw everything away because I don't know how to handle a problem. There is always a solution.

Life gets blurry at times, though. We might hear someone say, "I was having suicidal thoughts yesterday," and we think it's just a passing idea. Sometimes it is, but at other times, it's really a considered option coming from a darkness that activates within the person who made this statement. It is a danger zone.

Sometimes in life, there are times we don't see a way out of a situation. People who are at the breaking point in their lives and ready to kill themselves have concluded suicide is the only way out of their problem. It's as if they jump into a black hole, but each time they try to crawl out of the hole, instead of getting out, they end up slipping deeper and deeper. The only way to get out of the dark hole is by taking action and asking for help.

First and foremost, and with all my respect, I feel it necessary to write this chapter, because four times people who were suicidal called me for help. I am not a doctor or counselor, in any way, or an expert in this area. Believe me, I wish I knew or was ready to face a situation like this ahead of time. I did not feel ready at all, but life is a series of events we can't always control.

I always heard stories about suicide on television programs or read about it in the newspaper, but I never thought it would touch my life in this way. My heart provided the words and guided me in what to say to my friends. What helped me was my intuition. I put myself in their shoes because I had to understand their problems from their point of view. I had to feel the pain they felt so I could help them find the way out.

After my near-death experience and the other miraculous events described in this book, I started helping people and being kind to others as a lifestyle. I helped many people through a variety of problems, but I never expected to receive my first phone call from someone ready to end his life. Since that first person, three others called me. This was what my heart told me to tell them.

"Hello. Good evening, my friend. How are you doing? Are you okay? What's going on? It's late at night—is everything okay? Do you need help with something?"

They all responded that they wanted to take their lives.

So, I made sure they knew I was with them and I started asking the following questions:

1. What motivated you to call me and not your parents or someone else in your family?

They all said, the first name that came to their minds was Carlos. They were afraid of making their family feel bad. They thought their family wouldn't take them seriously and they would feel even more rejected. They wanted my opinion before they made their last move. Some of the people with whom I spoke to had tried to talk with their family, but the conversation did not go well.

2. Why do you want to take your life? What is your motivation to do that?

Their answer was, they were holding too much suffering and pain in their lives and that it didn't make any sense to continue living this way. They thought there was no other solution. Depression, confusion, guilt, escape from pain, financial problems, relationship problems, addiction, extreme loneliness, and of course a lack of faith were their main concerns. The bottom line was, they each felt nobody really cared and they didn't want to ask for help. The problems were all internalized and they didn't feel confident sharing them.

I said, "I know you don't see a way to escape, but give me a chance to help you and to make you understand that this not a solution. Give me the opportunity to show you that we can fix the problem you are facing now. Let's start over from the beginning. We can start with a prayer if you want. Let me give you my hand and let me help you to get out of this. Together we can do our best to fix it. I promise. I'm not going to give up on you. You have a brother here, and believe me, I care about you. That's what I'm here for."

They said, they thought it wouldn't matter if they were gone. Everyone would go about their lives as usual. I explained to them, committing suicide would create a ripple effect that will impact everybody around them for the rest of their lives. I explained they needed to think about their loved ones: their family, mom, dad, brothers or sisters, friends, coworkers, and everyone who surrounds them. A heavy stone would be left in their hearts forever.

3. In every religion I know, taking your own life is the worst thing you can do. It's a wrong thing. It's a sin. Think about that.

Remember what one of the oldest books on earth, the Bible, says in the verse, 1 Cor:6:19, the body is not our own.

4. Then, after a lot of talking with my friends about their situations in life, I close by asking them, "What are you are going to do now?"

I say, "Let me tell you something. You are valuable to this world. I'm here talking to you because I care for you. A lot of people love you, but people are busy with their lives, and nobody can stand behind you all the time, asking if you have a problem or how you are feeling. I believe we all have a reason why we exist. There is a purpose for every person. Why would you want to miss this amazing opportunity to be who you want and do anything you want? Even if you don't do it, at least you enjoy the ride in this fascinating game of life."

I believe life is a beautiful experience every human being needs to enjoy and appreciate with respect. Our lives are a blessing. Instead of ending your life, find another solution—that's when miracles can happen. People who go through this reach the rock bottom of their lives.

When we feel fear, we become frozen. Life is not easy. We have to face challenges and obstacles every day that we need to overcome—it's a part of life experience. Life is like a big school where we come to learn several lessons that will require us to be strong and have faith in the future. Some obstacles in my life have appeared to be as big as Mount Everest.

Remember when I had terminal cancer? How do you think I felt at the moment the doctor gave me the diagnosis? I felt terrible, but something inside of me said, *even though everything looks scary now, it will be fine.* My doctor told me I did not have long to live, yet I saw a light of hope at the end. How? I heard my inner voice and I asked myself this simple question, What if? What if a miracle happens? What if the doctor made a mistake? What if someway or somehow this can disappear or vanish out of the blue? Options are available, right? I didn't have any idea what I would do, but deep inside of me I knew I had to take action. When a problem starts to scale up and get as big as an iceberg, it's the fear that is really growing—the feeling of danger. It will paralyze you to the point where you can't even move because you can't see the way out.

The result is that the problem doesn't disappear. If we don't move or do something, it remains. For me, the best way to begin facing the problem is to write it down in the middle of a page and circle it. Then draw lines out, like a sun, and write possible solutions all around the problem. I then go to my computer and type my problem in the search bar. Believe me, you will find a lot of stories and solutions to your problem. If you think you can't face the problem by yourself, ask for help. Pray and meditate on how to solve this problem. Sometimes I talk to older people in their seventies, eighties, or nineties. I always ask, "If you were my age, what would you do?" They have plenty of life experience and have gathered more knowledge along the way. They have given me the magic answer I needed to move through the problem.

The biggest problems in my life were smaller than I thought, but my fear blew them out of proportion. When I was able to see the problem for what it was, I couldn't believe it had a simple solution. When we go through hard times, it's a way for us to grow. Hard times are an opportunity for us to listen to that small still voice inside of us, the one giving us the advice to reach our goals and be the best. We are trying to overcome, but we start trying to make sense of what this voice is trying to tell us. Sometimes, it doesn't make any sense, but we still have to follow that instinct. When we follow its guidance, we follow our heart, and everything falls in place in ways we never expected. Our consciousness knows the right thing to do.

When we completely surrender to our higher consciousness, we surrender to God. We hand our lives over to Him and feel freedom and relief from overseeing our lives and making a big mess of everything. When we surrender, we still have to work and be good people, but the suffering ends because we accept the help that was always there. We were just too stubborn or ignorant to see it. This is an opportunity for us to accept the love of God as the guiding hand in our lives.

When my friends called for help, I listened to my inner guidance. Through the use of my phone, I held their hands and showed them life is beautiful and there is a light at the end of their problem. The most important thing in those situations was that they asked for help. Please, if you are going through a difficult time, ask for help. Believe me, there is always somebody that will help you. Take action. Pick up the phone. Call someone you know who cares about you—a friend, colleague, significant other, cousin, aunt, or your parents. If they don't answer, call the National Suicide Prevention Lifeline at 1-800-273-8255 in the US or go to their website at www.suicidepreventionlifeline.org.

Give yourself another chance. Have faith and trust God. He has a plan for your life. I also will be here anytime you need me. Trust me everything will be all right.

CHAPTER 17

LOVE & GRATITUDE

———

There are so many people with an emptiness inside of them. It's like an empty cup we keep trying to fill with alcohol, too much work, drugs, crazy relationships, drama, and every kind of distraction. Those things will never fill the cup. What will fill that cup is love—real love, unconditional love.

To do volunteer work is better than any medication or therapy. It is a magical thing that is free. It has gifts in it that are waiting for you to discover. When we do volunteer work, we do it to simply give to others. It's work without pay. It's work other people may not even notice. There are no awards. It's just you and the work. You sign up. You commit to it. You show up and the work is usually very simple. Then something strange happens. Conversations that would not have happened elsewhere start to happen. Answers to our problems somehow arise. We start feeling connected, feeling we are putting value out in the world, even if it's while stuffing envelopes. Whenever I leave a volunteer experience, I leave with more than I came with.

My best example of the magic of volunteer work was something I saw once. A kid called his aunt and said he's had it. He can't go on anymore. He was going to run away or take his life. She calmed him down and said, "Look out your window. What do you see?" He described the area around his house.

She said, "Okay, you see the older woman, the neighbor, across the street? She has leaves on her front yard. Go get your rake. Don't knock on her door or anything. Just go over there and rake up all her leaves. Then call me back as soon as you are done."

He had nothing to lose. It didn't make any sense, but he did it anyway. He finished in no time and called her.

He said, "Wow! I can't believe it. How did that happen? It's such a strange thing. How can doing that simple easy thing make such a difference? I feel amazing. I feel like I can just talk to my family now and sort things out. While I was raking, I thought of what to say. What happened?"

This is service. Service is a spiritual practice anyone can do. When we join an organization we personally believe in and commit to a schedule, it's the best present we can give to ourselves. The empty cup gets filled over time. When we give to others, somehow the Golden Rule is activated, and we give to ourselves. The greatest gift we can give to others is the gift of our time.

Some of the volunteer work I have done in the past is feeding the homeless at Atlanta shelters, working with Toys for Tots, and helping at a home and summer camp for refugee children. Working at these places gave me a feeling of gratitude. It filled my heart with purpose, love, and satisfaction, which money can't buy. If you are empty inside, try to help a nonprofit organization and you will see what I'm talking about. I wish you the best in your journey to self-realization.

Through my journey with leukemia and my near-death experience, I realized I needed to abandon my old habits and create new ones that truly fill my life purpose and soul. I did not see it before. Now I see clearly. The new way I see everything is that I must respect this precious life that has been given to me.

I know my purpose now. In the depths of my heart, I can see clearly I am here to help others. I do not know how that will look and I am open to doing whatever I need to do. I will follow my inner guidance. I will follow the signs shown to me. I will listen to the people who give me messages I can feel are the right ones.

My life has a fresh start and I see things differently than I have ever before. I cannot waste any more time. I am redefining my life priorities. Every time I go to the beach, I feel amazing. With the sound of the waves, the breeze on my skin, the salty fragrance, and the sand under my feet, I have a full sensory experience that fulfills my needs.

I found out gratitude is one of the best practices I can do every day. I heard about it in different traditions, religions, and cultures, but I really didn't understand the concept. When I started searching and hearing people talk about gratitude, they said everything around them starts changing like magic. It is like we emit a vibration of love and thankfulness to the universe and it comes back to us in unexpected ways. I believe we as humans have life energy. When we start being thankful for everything we have today in life, I feel we send a signal, a vibration, to God saying, "Thank you. I'm grateful. Send me more."

It is a miracle to be alive and now that I have gone through these experiences, I see I have been given a second chance at life. I see the value of my life and how each day is a chance for me to show gratitude for the life I have. When I love myself and my life, I show respect to God who created me.

This story doesn't end here. It continues with you, dear reader. Now you have the power of the dolphin within you too. It will go with you wherever you go in life. The dolphins remind us to give love, harmony, and kindness to others and to be compassionate and grateful to every person who crosses our paths. Remember to enjoy life the best way you can. I send you many, many blessings for your life and I wish you all the best.

ACKNOWLEDGMENTS

——

I want to give special thanks, first to God, for giving me life because his Divine Presence has been in my life—every step, every chapter, every moment. He has taken care of me, even when I didn't recognize it and I couldn't see or understand what He wanted from me. I was skeptical. I was a slow learner and God was patient. He sent me so many messages until I finally could not deny His presence in my life. His way is the best way. It took years for me to catch on, but now I finally truly understand. I want to thank God for trusting me and giving me this opportunity to show others all my experiences, so they too can learn from them. Thank you for guiding me and showing me what I have to do. Thank you for bringing light, peace, and serenity to my life.

Thank you for life itself. I now understand a bit more about the meaning of life, about finding your gifts, and how the purpose of life is to give those gifts away. In my understanding, we have to enjoy the present moment: every second, every minute, every step, and most importantly, enjoying the company of others.

Thank you for each sunrise and sunset to bless the day, another gift I make a point of noticing. We have heaven on earth right here, but we are constantly distracted by exterior factors, news, TV, work, social media, and stress. One of the best discoveries I found is to disconnect from all this distraction and reconnect with mother earth. Enjoy the richness and beauty of nature by spending time, walking, and just observing the miracles of nature outside. Just sit quietly next to a river, a mountain, a lake, or in front of the ocean and observe the calmness and the beauty of nature and take a deep breath. Since these experiences, I have the gifts of gratitude and awareness. I have reprioritized my whole life. I am grateful for all I have, all I know, and all that is coming along my path, in my future life journey.

I am so grateful to my mom, Amarillys, for being such a strong a single parent and for raising me and my siblings. She was always on me to help me be a better person at every stage of my life. She was strict with me, preparing me for life. She taught me valuable things about life. I can still hear her regular sayings, such as: work for what you want, things are not free in life; you have to make it happen; whatever you do, do it right or don't do it; being humble can open all the doors; respect is the foundation of all good relationship; never cross the line or you will have regrets; integrity will let you sleep well each night of your life; there is no better place than home; family is the longest-lasting relationship—honor it the most.

The main thing I learned from her is that when a man stops being humble, he loses everything. Of course, every problem can be solved with the Golden Rule: Do unto others as you would have them do unto you. She even encouraged me to continue fighting for my dreams. When she was on her deathbed, her finals words were, "I'm your biggest fan and I will always be with you. I will be looking over you and protecting you from the other side. I will be waiting for you, from anywhere in the universe, God bless you." She closed her eyes very slowly and left this world, with a peaceful expression on her face. Thank you, God, for the gift of her last words.

Thank you to my dad, Carlos, for being as kind as Mother Teresa. He is the best dad in the world. He was Google before it even existed. He answered every question I had from age three until today. Even though my parents divorced when I was six years old, my dad always took care of me and my sister, checking on us. He was my inspiration. He was a pillar for me and the rest of my family. He had a humanitarian heart for everyone. He really understood his brothers and friends.

Many people who knew my dad sought him out for counsel. He loved to work. He would say, "Every job is honorable." He understood karma too and always said, "What goes around, comes around." He taught me a lot, including keeping your mind busy on healthy things so you don't get distracted by flashy things, and that God will grab you by the throat when you are off track but He won't squeeze the last breath out of you. He taught us moderation in all things and to help others as that way our hearts will be full of love and gratitude.

Thank you to my sister Jennifer, for being my second mom after my mother went to heaven, walking with me through my whole life, and taking care of me in every moment of my life. Thank you to my brother-in-law Raul Gil for all his advice in life. Thank you to my beautiful nieces, Shannon and Oriana, for being the best nieces I could dream of having.

Thank you to my friend Will, for always being there as the brother that life gave me.

Thank you to life, for giving me more brothers than I could ever ask for in William Nachreiner, Austin Thompson, Thomas Sawyer, Daniel Magdziarz, Dav Dau, Ramiro Salcido, Raul Gil, Jose Luis Marin, Douglas Pina, Pedro Pelaez, Juan Alfonso Baptista, Oscar Feo, Sean Hartman, Will Baily, Cesar Gonzalez, Victor Donado, Jorge Donado, Rene Mey, Frankie Rodriguez, Alain Diaz, and Guillermo Santana.

Thank you to Ursula, for being in my spiritual path when it started and continuing to help me on this long journey.

Thank you to Crystal, for being my mentor and my guide.

Thank you to Haydee, Edgar, Sofia, and Vanessa, for letting me be part of your family.

Thank you to Joyce Rennolds, for being a beautiful soul who enlightened my spiritual path as the sweetest teacher ever.

Thank you to Tatianna Gamma and Julia Chacon, for being the most beautiful people at the beginning of my career on television.

Thank you to Lourdes Martinez, Yuly Rivas, Tatiana, Maria Deangel and Josibel, Gigi Dancourt, Adriana Feo, Krystel Sanchez, Valentina Palacios, Justina M Grinholc, Tatiana Da Gama, Gaby Mendez, Genesis Mendez, Janet Vieira, Anilu Fiz and Valerie Alino, for being the sisters life gave me.

Thank you to my spiritual mothers, Maria Espinal, Luz Maria, Nancy de Gimenez, Miriam Carlotti, Ivonne Chirinos, Nancy Hamburger, Angelica Avila, Haydee Pelaez, Teresa Ramos, Ines Baptista, Marcella Morelli, Teresa Zoraida, Luisa, Gladys, Albertina Yokoshi, Arianna Mendez, Rita Vieira, Maria Concepcion Moleros, Julia Chacon, Edivette, Yuraima Pineda, Crystal, and Joyce Rennolds.

Special thanks to:

Willian Nachreiner, Jose Luis Marin, Ursula Lentine, Paulina Rangel, Nicole Dominguez, Brett Belcastro, Miguel

Corral, Rachel Mc Gehee, Julie Thomas, Eduardo Gimenez, Bert Rothkugel, James Hoskins, Linda Edwards, Shannon Lane Corbertt, David Rogers, Ramiro Salcido, Will Bailey, Vanessa Pelaez, Nolan Ryan Byrnes, Tracey Owens Lowd, Bartholomew Perez, Nella Ancheta, Jenniffer Carrasquel, Corey Jacobs, Shannon Gil, Jana Tarnovska, Vijaya Muntha, Alain Diaz, Orianna Gil, Maki Manning, Jorge Cabrera Lima, Pilar Verdes, Daniel Magdziarz, Amanda Hester, Sara Bremer, Buck Moore, Juliana Henao, Justyna M. Grinholc, Laura Rachel, Eric Koester, Michael Barnhill, Melissa Oliver, Nicole Hardy Mizoguchi , Rita Janeen Minster, and Joyce Rennolds.

I would also like to give a big thank you to the person who came into my life to help me edit my book. Thank you to Sandy Huffman, for being the light that illuminated my path through this process. Even though we were in different states and we communicated via Zoom calls, you were always there any time I needed your help. Thank you for being a good friend and bringing your knowledge to make my book digestible for the audiences.

Lastly, I would like to thank all the people who made this dream possible and helped me with my book campaign. You are like bright stars on my path to creating, *Help from Heaven*. I'm not going to name all of you but know I love you guys a lot. If I start listing messages one by one, I will have to write a new book. Hugs to everyone and I hope you enjoyed my story.

APPENDIX

———

CHAPTER 7

Animal Welfare Institute. "Report: 100,000+ Dolphins, Small
Whales and Porpoises Slaughtered Globally Each Year." Animal Welfare Institute press release, August 7, 2018. Animal
Welfare Institute website. https://awionline.org/press-releases/
report-100000-dolphins-small-whales-and-porpoises-slaugh-
tered-globally-each-year, accessed June 26, 2021.

Brewster, B. Chris, Richard E. Gould, and Robert W. Brander.
"Estimations of rip current rescues and drowning in the United
States." Natural Hazards and Earth System Sciences 19, no. 2
(February 2019): 389-397. https://doi.org/10.5194/nhess-19-389-
2019, accessed June 26, 2021.

CHAPTER 8

Blackshear, Thomas and Roy Lessin. *Forgiven*. Colorado Springs,
CO: Chariot Victor Pub., 1996.

CHAPTER 9

Georgia Bulletin Staff. "Superior general's Atlanta visit inspires Missionaries of Charity community." The Georgia Bulletin, August 8, 2019. https://georgiabulletin.org/news/2019/08/superior-generals-atlanta-visit-inspires-missionaries-of-charity-community/.

Mother Teresa of Calcutta Center. "Mother Teresa of Calcutta Biography." Accessed June 26, 2021. https://motherteresa.org/biography.html.

CHAPTER 10

Gould, Wendy Rose. "What Are Sound Baths? The Healing Power of Sound." Very Well Mind. Accessed June 2021. https://www.verywellmind.com/what-are-sound-baths-4783501.

CHAPTER 13

Pure Vida Bracelets. "Save the Dolphins Bracelet." Accessed June 26, 2021. https://www.puravidabracelets.com/products/save-the-dolphins.

CHAPTER 15

Rennolds, Joyce. "Wisdom: Scripting – Connecting With Infinite Possibilities." Accessed June 26, 2021. http://joycerennolds.com/wisdom.htm.